Favorite
New England
Airports

A Guide to Aviation Activities
and Entertainment

James S. Kohn, M.D.

PETER E. RANDALL PUBLISHER
PORTSMOUTH, NH•1998

Design and maps: Tom Allen

Cover; courtesy *Basin Harbor Club, Vergennes, VT*

Peter E. Randall Publisher
Box 4726
Portsmouth, NH 03802-4726

Contents

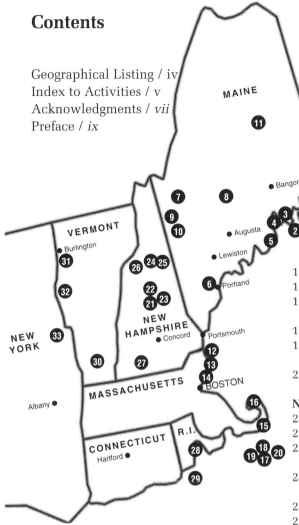

Geographical Listing of Airports

State   Airfield   Alternate Nmae   (Identifier)   Region

Maine

Bar Harbor	Hancock Co.	(BHB)	Coastal - Mid
Bethel	Col. Dyke	(OB 1)	Central Mtns.
Blue Hill		(07B)	Coastal - Mid
Bingham	Gadabout Gaddis	(Private)	Central
Isleboro		(57B)	Coastal - Mid
Millinocket		(MLT)	Central Mtns.
Portland		(PWM)	Coastal-South
Rangeley		(8B0)	Central-North
Rockland	Knox County	(RKD) (93B)	Coastal - Mid
Sugarloaf		(B21)	No. Central Mtns

Massachusetts

Bedford	Hanscom	(BED)	Boston
Beverly		(BVY)	North Shore
Chatham		(CQX)	Cape Cod-Mid
Katama Edgartown		(1B2)	Martha's Vineyard
Nantucket		(ACK)	Nantucket Island
Plum Island	Newburyport	(2B2)	North Shore
Provincetown	Race Point	(PVC)	Cape Cod - "Tip"
Tradewinds		(Private)	Martha's Vineyard
Vineyard Haven		(MVY)	Martha's Vineyard

New Hampshire

Franconia		(1B5)	White Mtns.
Jaffrey	Silver Ranch	(AFN)	South Central
Laconia		(LCI)	Lakes Region
Moultonboro		(NH08)	Lakes Region
Mt. Washington	Whitefield	(HIE)	White Mtns.
Twin Mountain		(8B2)	White Mtns.
Wolfeboro-Lakes Region		(8B8)	Lakes Region

New York

Warren Co.	Glens Falls	(GFL)	Upstate - Lake George

Rhode Island

Block Island		(BID)	Block Island
Newport State		(2B4)	Coastal

Vermont

Basin Harbor	Vergennes	(B06)	Lake Champlain
Burlington		(BTV)	Lake Champlain
Mount Snow	West Dover	(4V8)	South Central

Index to activities

continued on next page

Hiking/walking/climbing

Franconia
Twin Mountain
Millinocket
Bar Harbor
Laconia
Bethel

Horseback riding

Franconia
Jaffrey

Gliding/soaring (rides for hire)Bar Harbor
Franconia

Museums

Hanscom/Bedford (De Cordova -
        Sculpture)
Rockland (Farnsworth - Art,
        Owls Head - Transportation)
Franconia (Robert Frost)
Portland (Portland Museum of Art)

Rafting (whitewater)

Bingham
Millinocket

Skiing (downhill)

Sugarloaf (Sugarloaf Mountain)
Bethel (Sunday River area)
West Dover (Mt. Snow)
Burlington (several)
Laconia (Gunstock Mountain)

Skiing (touring)

Laconia
Moultonboro
Bar Harbor
Rangeley
Mount Washington
Franconia

Tennis (resorts)

Franconia (Franconia Inn)
Rockland (Samoset)
Vergennes (Basin Harbor)
Tradewinds (Farm Neck)
Glens Falls (Sagamore)

Acknowledgments

I would like to thank a few people who helped make this publication possible. The first is my transcriptionist, Michelle Swank, who typed the guide through the duration of her first pregnancy. Second is Peter Randall, whose resourcefulness brought the project to fruition. Third are those people who trusted me as pilot and friend in order that I could share these wonderful days.

Finally, I would like to acknowledge Dr. Jeremy Morton. He is a cardiac surgeon at the top of his field who took me flying one Sunday afternoon after we finished a triple bypass procedure. We went up the coast of Maine (Down East) to the Owls Head Transportation Museum and he let me fly, first from the right seat and then from the left. After that I was hooked. That was my first flight in a single-engine aircraft, and I have been flying ever since.

Preface

This guide is the result of travels and adventures, but, it was borne out of necessity. Being a native of Boston, I have always been partial to the splendor of the seasons-the beauty and variation of New England landscapes. During my second year of surgical residency in Portland, Maine, it became evident that my ability to travel New England was profoundly limited by time. On my one afternoon a week "off call," I became obsessed with escaping and exploring the coast, the mountains, and the countryside of this region where I was raised but had really experienced so little of. I took to flying for the same reasons that many others have: It fulfilled my quest for adventure, freedom, and challenge, and efficiently minimized travel time for certain trips. Each trip was transformed into an adventure as a result of my newly developed skills as a private pilot. I enjoyed the feeling of weightlessness, as well as the discipline of navigating and the technical aspects of flying. At my destination, I was intent on the pursuit of exercise and activity, since I often had to sacrifice these interests during a busy week at the hospital. This guide is, therefore, about flying to a place and about activity when you get there.

There is such a wide variety of activities presented here that I am sure people of all ages and interests will find use in it. Cycling, hiking, skiing, fishing, golfing, and swimming my way first along the Maine coast, the challenge was to combine these activities into a single aviation excursion on a weekly basis and to experience as much as possible in a given day. The sense of escape to an often remote area added appeal as well. As my confidence in flying and traveling evolved and my adventure-seeking behavior developed, I began to compile a series of what I termed "flying adventures." As my resourcefulness and exploration skills sharpened, I began to venture farther from coastal Maine, my home base.

Returning to Portland after each flying adventure, I felt as if I had traveled worlds away and left the frustrations of patient care and urban living long enough that I could take a fresh approach to problems. This was my way of surviving the stresses of five years of surgical internship and residency. I was rejuvenated after each trip and ready to pour my efforts into another week with patients.

Finally came the mature feeling of wanting to share these adventures with others so as to alleviate some of the organizational burden and minimize the "legwork" of planning a trip. Preparation is essential when flying, and small inconveniences are avoided with sound, specific, and strategic advice. This guide affords the reader more time for preparing the flight plan and weather assessment and less worry about those logistical details that remain more constant, like accommodations and activities and natural resources. Very often the success of an entire trip is made by a momentary breathtaking view or an invigorating hike or the acquisition of a special antique. I believe that this guide will help you make the most out of each flying experience you set out on; and more important, it will serve as a source for new ideas on this concept. This guide suggests how to do it. In many cases, you may have heard of these places and intended to go. Now is your time! Following a general plan is not the same as tracing someone's else's footsteps. You can use this guide in any capacity, as a simple blueprint for general ideas or to rely on the maps and trail guides provided for specific information and activities. An adventure is your own when you are the pilot in command.

When I return to some of my favorite places, I am always impressed that the very same spot yields a different experience from season to season. This small corner of the country has so much to offer in a condensed area. When multiplied by the four seasons, the possibilities for exploration and discovery are virtually limitless. With this variation in terrain and atmospheric conditions comes the need for specialized flying skills, knowledge, and judgment. Respect for mountainous terrain, summer convective activity, and winter icing, to name a few perils, is a necessity. Pick and choose your days carefully and ask your flying buddies for advice. I have yet to meet a pilot who was reluctant to share ideas about a place he had been to. You are probably aware that we are, as General Aviation (GA) pilots, a fraternal organization that by and large helps each other.

I once bought a big encyclopedia-type guide to entertainment at and around nearby U. S. airports. I found that the Aircraft Owners and Pilots Association (AOPA) directory was more helpful than that book I had paid $30 for. It was really nothing more than a list of nearby hotels and restaurants. In most cases, the author had never been to the establishments listed.

You are about to read a compilation of 33 wonderful days, not a list of airport restaurants. Use this guide to complement the AOPA directory and Airport Facilities Directory (AFD) to make the most of your trips.

The following is not intended to be a comprehensive list of activities covering all of New England; but rather, it is a selective guide to numerous wonderful days that I have experienced in the region. May it help you pursue your flying adventures with safety, confidence, and enthusiasm, and lead you to exciting aviation excursions all your own.

Please write to me with your questions, comments, and any new adventures you may have experienced. In some cases, the references or phone numbers may have changed since publication of this guide. I apologize for any inconvenience these changes may cause the reader.

Equipment for the Aviation Adventurer

The most valuable advice I can give on the subject of a successful trip is some preflight rudimentary planning. Often a quick call to the airport Fixed Base Operator (FBO), restaurant, operations desk, or nearby hotel will help you achieve this. Ask about courtesy cars, shuttle service, and accessible activities, in addition to those I have listed. The people who work there welcome transient pilots-helping people is their business and we make their day interesting.

I have a lot of toys—in-line skates, folding bikes, inflatable-rafts, to name a few. These have enabled me, in some cases, to venture far from small and remote airfields, as well as to stay fit. The Dahon folding (20 inch wheel) bicycles can fit in the rear compartment (behind the rear seat) of a Cessna 182 or 172. Two road bikes or mountain bikes can fit on the rear seat of a 182, if you take the rear wheels off. Don't be afraid of this, just carry a pair of garden gloves so that handling the chain doesn't become a mess. A large drop cloth is similarly a good idea to protect the inside of your plane from grease and road dirt. Other items that I found come in handy are:

- Cell phone
- Weather radio
- Bungee cords
- First aid kit
- Ropes
- Good flashlight
- Basic tool kit
- Blanket
- Luggage valet
- Tie- down Stake
- "Jumper" cables (if applicable to your aircraft)

—James S. Kohn, M.D.
35 Lapland Rd.
Chestnut Hill, MA 02467

MAINE

Sand Beach, Bar Harbor.

Bar Harbor (BHB)

Location: Down East coastal Maine, 4 hours' drive from Portland on Mount Desert Island

Airfield: Hancock County Bar Harbor Airport is really in Trenton, just across a small bridge from Mount Desert Island. The airfield has multiple instrument approaches and excellent facilities for its size and for the amount of use it gets. Most people recognize that so much money has been put into this airport because of the famous people who use it on occasion-the Rockefellers, Caspar Weinberger, for example. The runways are well maintained, smooth-surfaced, and relatively long and wide. Although the approach is adjacent to Cadillac Mountain, this is not a difficult airport to land at. The people at Acadia Air, a local FBO, are courteous, kind, and helpful. In the wintertime, they will hangar your plane overnight for a minimal charge, and warm it for your return flight. Ask for Tina at Acadia Air. She will give you invaluable advice.

Activities:
1. Gliding/soaring
2. Mountain biking (all levels)
3. Ocean and lake swimming
4. Sea kayaking
5. Hiking and mountain climbing
6. Eating lobsters

Background: Hancock County Bar Harbor is one of my favorite trips. I like to go in any season and find new adventure each time. Renting a car from the airport is easy and efficient. Accommodations are plentiful and range from camping to the most luxurious of New England inns. The list of activities is endless, and with the exception of the main town, Bar Harbor, this place really never gets crowded, even in the high summer season.

This is coastal Maine at its best. Crashing waves along the rocky shore yield some dramatic scenery. Somes Sound at Southwest Harbor, one of the inlets on this island, is the only natural fjord in this part of the country. You can see it best by air or boat, although hiking along the adjacent ridges is possible. Although I have never done it, many people enjoy gliding or soaring from this airport, and the rates are reasonable. I cannot think of a more beautiful place to experience a first glider ride than Mount Desert Island, with its views of the ocean, mountains, and lakes. Sea kayaking has gained increasing popularity over the last several years. Several outfits in Bar Harbor offer instruction, rentals, and guided tours. This is an ideal place to learn basic skills or to start an afternoon or weekend trip.

Acadia National Park occupies most of Mount Desert Island, and the beauty of this place is extremely well maintained and preserved. Carriage paths-(dirt roads leading through the park)-make cycling, walking, or running an absolute pleasure. Rarely will you see a horse-drawn carriage on the paths, although they were originally cut for them. These roads wind through the woods by lakes and up onto ridges from which you can see Cadillac Mountain and ocean views in the same vista. The paths are lined with blueberry bushes in August. I love this place and come here at least two or three times a year.

If You Go:
Rent a car from Hancock County Bar Harbor Airport and find a secluded country inn. Or take a cab into Bar Harbor and stay at an inn on one of the quiet side streets. I have done both. This is one of the few places where I have never had problems getting a room even on the busiest of weekends. At several places in town, bicycles are free for guests. Take a hybrid or mountain bike onto the carriage paths starting at the park entrance closest to Bar Harbor and travel down to Seal Harbor. Here, there is a beach and a delicatessen where you can make a picnic lunch. After lunch and a dip in the refreshing Maine waters, you can take a nap on the village green, just between the beach and the deli. Find a shady spot and forget about all the frustrations of the past week. On your way back, cycle past Eagle Lake to Bar Harbor and then home.

If you choose to rent a car and want to see an especially beautiful part of the island, drive towards Southwest Harbor and look for signs marked ST. SAVEUR. These signs will be just opposite the sign for Echo Lake recreational area. Take a short hike up St. Saveur Trail, which overlooks Somes Sound. Bring a picnic lunch and some good walking shoes. This is neither a technical climb nor a lengthy walk. Total time up should take you about an hour ; to descend a little bit more than half that.

Finally, if you want to do some of the more touristy activities, which involve less exercise, take a drive by Thunder Hole and Sand Beach on Loop Road, just outside the town of Bar Harbor. You can

Bar Harbor (BHB)

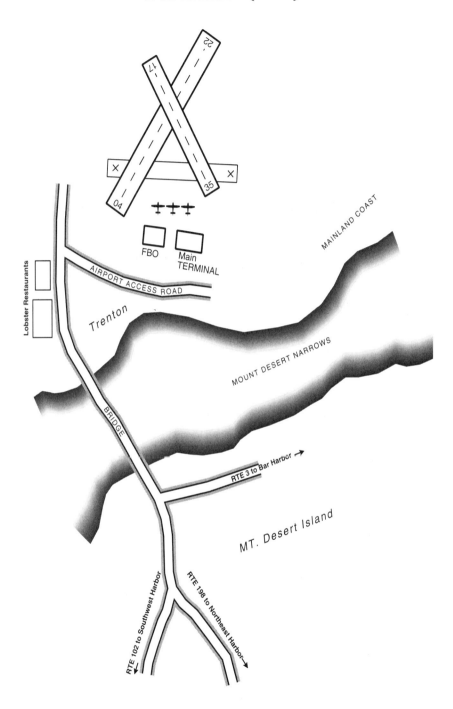

gain beautiful views from your car at a variety of lookout points. Across Sand Beach, a number of walking trails are perfect for those low-impact afternoons. If you have the need for climbing, the Bee Hive is a strenuous 2-hour ascent up Cadillac Mountain. All this is accessible from Loop Road for a single entry fee. This is the most heavily populated tourist area on Mount Desert Island, but well worth seeing for the first-time visitor to Bar Harbor and Acadia National Park.

Contacts:
Bar Harbor Chamber of Commerce will send you a free guide of this area. Their address is:
Bar Harbor Chamber of Commerce
    (207) 288-5103 or (800) 288-5103
    93 Cottage Street
    Bar Harbor, 04609

Briar Field Inn (free bicycles for guests)
    (207) 288-5297or (800) 228-6660
    64 Cottage Street, Bar Harbor, 04609

Kingsleigh Inn (open year round)
    (207) 244-5302
    P.O. Box 593, Main Street
    Southwest Harbor, 04679
    (Innkeepers have offered transportation to and from the airport in the off-season.)

Coastal Kayaking Tours
    (207) 288-9605 or (800) 526-8615
    48 Cottage Street
    Bar Harbor, 04609

Bar Harbor Bicycle Shop (in town). Maps of the carriage paths are available here.
    (207) 288-3886
    141 Cottage Street
    Bar Harbor, 04609

Acadia Air (FBO and Soaring/Gliding)
    (207) 667-5534

Islesboro (57B)

Location: Islesboro is an island, 14 miles long, located on Penobscot Bay, 3 miles from the mainland.

Airfield: The airfield is a 2400-foot x 50-foot paved runway. There are no facilities at the field, and there is no FBO. The approach to runway 01 is challenging because of surrounding trees, especially in gusty winds, though not prohibitively so. First, find the island by its shape on your VFR chart and then head for its center-you can't miss the strip!

Activities:
1. Golfing
2. Cycling
3. Walking
4. Escaping

Background: Islesboro is true and unspoiled Down East Maine. You will never encounter crowds here, even on the most beautiful summer day. The community is somewhat closed, and you'll always be a tourist, so don't even try and disguise yourself to this native population of 200 winter residents and 800 summer inhabitants. Topographically, the island is beautiful with many coves, rocky shores, and a few beaches. There is one main town and one inn. This is a place to get away to, slow down, and even travel back a couple of decades. Most people reach the island by ferry. During the summer, nine scheduled trips daily leave from Lincolnville to reach the island. The airfield gets very little use, so consider yourself, once again, one of the privileged few to gain access by air!

Recently, the island has gained some publicity, as two movie stars have discovered it. John Travolta and Kirstie Alley have summer residences here. Fortunately, they seem to enjoy the island for its natural treasures and take care to preserve its low-profile image. Neither of them seems to be interested in hosting extravaganzas or publicizing their daily routine, and people seem to respect their privacy. John Travolta usually flies into Portland International Jetport on a private jet and hires a helicopter to complete the trip to Islesboro.

For such a small island, 14 miles long and just a few miles wide, the topography is interesting and varied. The main road, which runs north-south, is notable for a few steep hills and is an invigorating bicycle tour. Much of the island is heavily wooded, with small farms interspersed. While there is only one main town, there are several small stores along the main road for the cyclist or walker seeking refreshments.

If You Go:

Islesboro is a place to slow down for a day or two, with someone special. Clearly, for an aviation adventure, you must time it right. This is a VFR airport in coastal Maine, which threatens some of the most solid IFR weather conditions in all seasons. To play it safe, make alternative plans to rent a car from Rockland, Knox County Regional Airport, which has multiple instrument approaches and lengthy runways. In this way, you may not have to cancel your trip should you decide on an overnight stay at Islesboro. You could alternatively fly to Rockland then drive to Lincolnville and take the ferry to Islesboro.

The Dark Harbor House, Islesboro's charming inn, is booked most weekends during the summer months. Here you will find wonderful Maine hospitality. These people are innkeepers because they love it. They enjoy meeting their guests and are dedicated to making your stay a memorable one. If you call them, they will send you a brochure, describing each individual room. With some planning, you can make the most of your overnight or weekend. Tell them your ideas about activities. Bicycles are available at the inn, and golf at a private course can be arranged. Private boat cruises can also be arranged. The innkeepers are willing and happy to help you plan.

I suggest a cycle tour around the island or of at least one end of it. This is a nice way to experience the island at a leisurely pace, and this may be all you want to do during your stay on Islesboro.

Contacts:

Dark Harbor House
  (207) 734-6669

Maine State Ferry Service
  (207) 789-5611

  (from Rockland, Maine)
  (207) 734-6935

Rental car from Rockland/Knox Co. Regional Airport
  (207) 594-5275

Islesboro (57B)

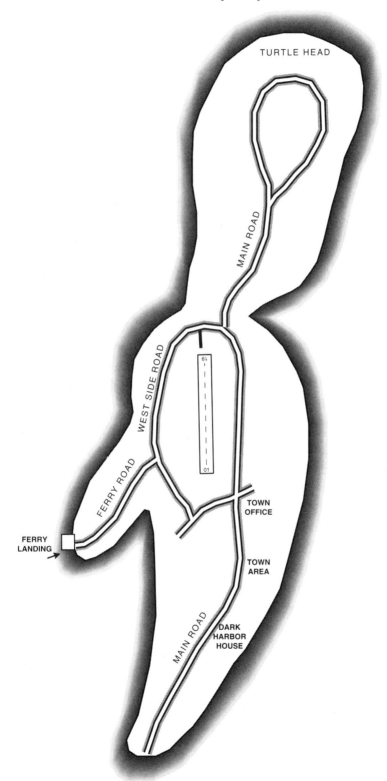

Stonington (93B)

Location: Coastal Maine, Penobscot Bay, at the tip of Deer Isle

Airfield: Stonington sits at the tip of Deer Isle, an island in Penobscot Bay connected to the mainland by a bridge. This is another place that is quite tedious to travel to by car, yet perfectly accessible to the GA pilot when satisfactory weather conditions prevail. You will never find crowds here, in fact, when you read that this airport is unattended, you had better count on it! The landing strip was repaved in 1994 and is now in reasonable condition. It is relatively short and narrow, but the approach is open and straightforward. Once again, there are no airport services and not much activity around the field. Self-sufficiency and arranged transportation are key here.

Activities:
1. Cycling
2. Antique and craft shopping
3. Exploring the Maine coast

Background: Stonington is an unspoiled coastal area, free of crowds at any time of year. The pace is slow and, in many ways, you may feel about 15 years behind the times. The roads in this area are beau-

Stonington (93B)

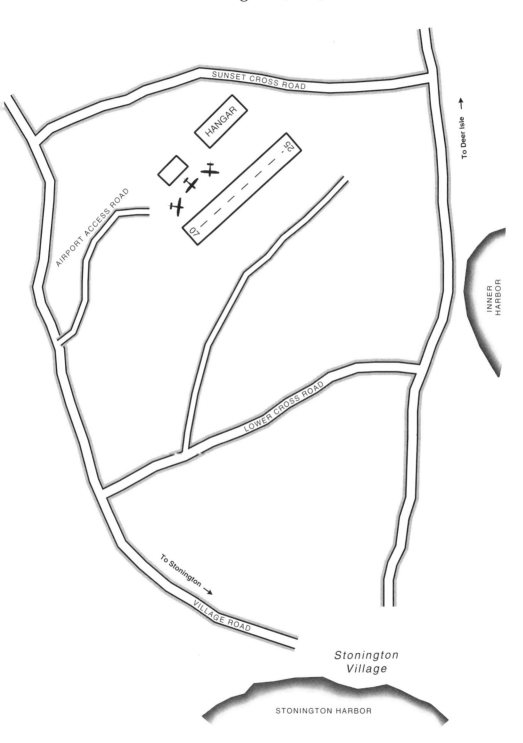

tiful and wind through a variety of inlets and coves. A few small villages are scattered at convenient intervals, making it easy to stop every half hour at an antique shop, restaurant, or country store. There are several bed & breakfasts, country inns, and small hotels. This is less of a resort area and more of a place to relax and "take in" coastal Maine.

If You Go:
Fly to Stonington on a summer or early fall day. Bring your own chocks or tie-down stakes. There are plenty of places to park, but only a few have tie-down ropes.

The Pilgrim's Inn is a beautiful bed & breakfast approximately 5 miles from the airfield. The innkeepers will fetch you, upon arrival, if you call ahead to arrange this. The inn is simple and elegant, and they offer home-cooked meals to guests, both breakfast and dinner. If you do not bring your own bicycles, they will supply them, free of charge. Although there are no protected bike paths, the main roads are not busy, and this is a wonderful way to travel the area. The inn is situated on a private cove and has splendid views and grounds. It is the perfect place to spend a couple of days; bona fide stress management! The innkeepers are dedicated to helping you achieve a memorable weekend and will prearrange other activities for you, such as sailing, golf, tennis, cycling, and hiking. If you sit down with them at cocktail hour, you will learn about the treasures of this enchanted corner of Maine. My favorite thing to do is to cycle along these country roads, stopping at the various coves to look out at the scenic coastline.

Another adventure worth embarking on is to take the mail boat to the Isle au Haut, several miles off the coast of Stonington, which leaves from the town harbor. Enjoy yourself, as you will experience Down East Maine in the way that few others care to.

Contacts:
Pilgrims Inn
    (207) 348-6615
    Deer Isle, 04627

Stonington Airport (information)
    (207) 367-2351

Blue Hill (07B)

Location: Blue Hill is a coastal town on Penobscot Bay, south of Mount Desert Island and north of Camden.

Airfield: The field is a 3000-foot grass strip, which may be a bit difficult to find given that the coastline is so jagged and the area so rural. The VFR approach is fairly easy for a soft field surrounded by trees and hills. No significant services are available at this field. It is very quiet here.

Activities:
1. Relaxation
2. Gourmet dining
3. Blueberry picking

Background: An older surgeon friend of mine, who has traveled widely throughout the coastal region of the state, once told me that Blue Hill is the prettiest town in Maine. This place is completely unspoiled by crowds, tourists, and commercial activity. This is a relaxing weekend or a day trip for the person who appreciates beautiful landscapes, fine food, and the essence of coastal Maine. There are two or three top-rated bed & breakfasts here, and two restaurants in town that offer gourmet dining. I am not sure how they do it, for this town gives new meaning to the term "sleepy," even in high summer. One afternoon I sat beneath some fur trees on public property in town and thought about what I wanted to do over the next 20 years. When I want to implement stress management these days, I recreate this scene in my mind.

Transportation from the airport can be a problem if you want to have a car with you. On the other hand, this is not entirely necessary, as the inns listed below will offer airport transport to their guests. I use my foldable bicycle when traveling to Blue Hill Airport, an easy 3-mile jaunt to town. There is even a convenience store on the way for refreshments, information, or directions. When you get to town, you'll see restaurants, antiques stores, and, most impressively the beautiful harbor, but don't blink because it's one short cluster along the main street!

Blue Hill (07B)

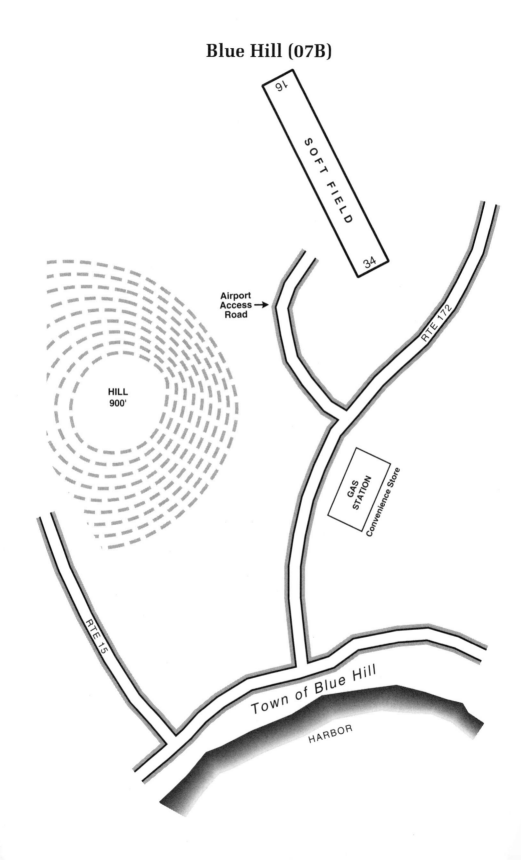

If You Go:
Travel to Blue Hill on a VFR summer day, mid-season. Make reservations at the John Peters Inn and have someone pick you up at the field. Ask the innkeepers to make a dinner reservation for you, if you are coming on a weekend. Rent a canoe and paddle around the harbor in town or just sit by the banks of the shore and do nothing. This is about the best place I have ever been to do just that, nothing. When you return to the airfield, before you go home, I suggest you embark on a blueberry-picking expedition. You won't have to go far, because the edges of the runway are lined with blueberry bushes. One day I collected a bag in about 20 minutes. This is a sport the whole family can enjoy during most of August.

Contacts:
John Peters Inn
>   (207) 374-2116
>   Peters Point
>   Blue Hill, 04614

The Blue Hill Inn
>   (207) 374-2844
>   Maine Street and Route 177
>   Blue Hill, 04614

Rockland (RKD)

Location: Coastal Maine, Penobscot Bay

Airfield: Knox County Regional Airport
    This airport is user-friendly, even for the most inexperienced general aviation pilots. The runways are wide and long, and the approaches are clear of difficult obstacles or terrain.

Activities:
1.   Owls Head Transportation Museum (on field)
2.   Farnsworth Museum (Wyeth Collection)
3.   Sailing (Camden Harbor)
4.   Windjammer Cruises
5.   Golf (Samoset Resort)

Background: A trip to Rockland, offers a variety of activities. For the aviation history buff, the Owls Head Transportation Museum is a must. It features an outstanding collection of antique automobiles, motorcycles, and planes. The displays are extremely well done and educational. The museum is located right at the airfield next to an aviation tie-down area. It usually closes around 4 P.M. on weekends, so call ahead to be sure it's open.

The approach into Rockland is quite picturesque, and it is easy to understand why a walking trail has been established around the airport area. Venturing away from the Knox County Airfield, the town of Rockland is only 4 to 5 miles. Taxi service is available and the local FBO can have a cab waiting for you upon landing. This is Down East hospitality and should not go unrecognized. You will find it almost everywhere you go in coastal Maine, and it makes flying here pleasurable, and stress free.

The town of Rockland is known as a workingman's port. In contrast with its neighbor, Camden, which is a haven for summer yachtsmen, Rockland has rustic charm. The restaurants feature honest, Down East cooking with less emphasis on presentation. Nevertheless, wonderful bed & breakfasts as well as seaside dining are available. The Farnsworth Museum is in the town of Rockland, featuring some of the finer works of Winslow Homer and Andrew Wyeth. Rockland is also the headquarters of Outward Bound, the renowned personal development and survival institution.

Rockland (RKD)

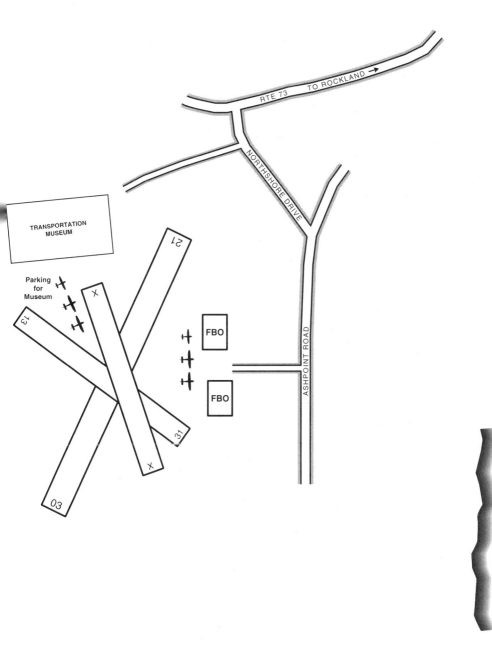

The breakwater at Samoset Resort, Rockland, ME

To tour the area, I would suggest renting a car from the local FBO, Downeast Air. Camden is about a 15-minute drive. This town is full of boutiques, antiques, and retail items for the discriminating shopper. I recommend Cappy's for a hearty, pub-style lunch. The summer community is best known for its sailboat-racing enthusiasts. In winter, the Camden Snow Bowl serves as coastal Maine's only downhill skiing opportunity. The views are tremendous, and the hill is never crowded. This is a wonderful afternoon of exercise for the beginner to intermediate skier.

If You Go:
My two favorite days, starting from Knox County Regional Airport, are as follows: I take three of my closest friends to brunch at the Samoset Resort. The Samoset is a lovely place, approximately 7 miles from the airfield, which I usually access by taxi. The people at the hotel are almost always willing to give my guests and me a ride back in their courtesy van. It's a good idea to go easy on meals for three days prior to the brunch. This is one of the best values you'll ever have, at approximately $15 for all you can eat. There is often shrimp and salmon, and even Lobster Newburg, and the dessert table is equally impressive. This is a gastronomic exercise that should not be underestimated. The meal starts at noon and goes until 2 P.M.

After brunch, we usually take a walk on the breakwater, which leads almost a full mile out into Penobscot Bay. This breakwater has a long history and took many years to build. At its base, it is over 100 feet wide, and when dry is a safe and comfortable walk for almost anyone. I have found that this postprandial activity alleviates some of the guilt associated with overeating.

For accommodations, I have two recommendations: The first is the Samoset, particularly in the off-season. It offers free shuttle service to and from the airfield with a comfortable and spacious courtesy van. The resort is perfect for a family outing in its scope of activities and facilities, but private enough for a romantic getaway as well.

Closer to the town of Rockland, down one of the quiet side streets, is the LimeRock Inn. This is a Victorian inn, reasonably priced, especially in the off-season, with a great deal of charm and two very gracious hosts. By calling ahead, you can arrange for a lovely afternoon on Penobscot Bay with your friends in a 40-foot sailboat. Thom, the owner and innkeeper, will be your captain. He is a veteran sailor and offers this outing as a unique opportunity to his guests. Penobscot Bay has international acclaim for its sailing, with many private coves and interesting places to stop along the dramatic coastline. For the sailing enthusiast, this is a convenient opportunity to charter a comfortable boat with an experienced captain. The LimeRock Inn is just a short walk to the Farnsworth Museum and to Rockland's main street.

Contacts:

Samoset Resort
    (207) 594-2511 or (800) 341-1650
    220 Warrenton Street
    Rockport, 04856

William A. Farnsworth Library and Art Museum
    (207) 596-6457
    19 Elm Street
    Rockland, 04841

The LimeRock Inn
    (207) 594-2257 or (800) 546-3762
    96 Limerock Street
    Rockland, 04841

Owls Head Transportation Museum
    (207) 594-4418

Downeast Air at Knox County Regional Airport
   (207) 594-2171

Penobscot Air Service (FBO)
   (800) 780-6071

Portland, Maine (PWM)

Location: Coastal Maine, a 1 1/2-hour drive north of Boston

Airfield: Portland International Jetport is an ideal destination for the weekend adventurer. It has all the amenities and facilities of a major international airport, yet it is user-friendly to the general aviation pilot. At Northeast Air, you can usually obtain a courtesy car for day use, especially when you call ahead. Car rental from the major agencies is also easy and reliable. Portland Jetport offers a variety of precision and nonprecision approaches, and the traffic is quite manageable, even for the student pilot. The controllers are friendly, and this is really a great place to learn and to practice mixing it up with "the big guys," private and commercial jet aircraft pilots. The runways are long and wide, and the airport layout is very straightforward. Northeast Air is the FBO closest to the main terminal and rental car agencies.

Activities:
1. Shopping
2. Walking
3. Hiking
4. Dining

Background: Portland is well known to the native New Englander, but few people enjoy it to its full potential. The old port, Portland's historic waterfront district, has some great restaurants and shopping with a distinct local flavor. It lies 4 miles from the jetport.

Approximately 7 miles from the jetport is one of my favorite spots, Two Lights State Park. This area of Cape Elizabeth has some beautiful rock formations and a nice shore-side path to walk along. The Maine coast is quite dramatic in this region, and Two Lights is a perfect place to experience this during a leisurely walk.

If you want to do some power shopping, L. L. Bean sits right

Portland (PWM)

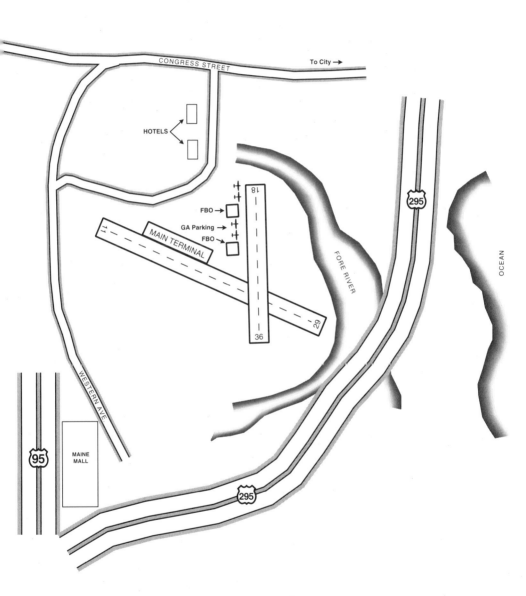

in the heart of Freeport, a mecca for outlet stores. Freeport is a 20-minute drive from the airport, straight up Route 295 northbound.

Another short drive from Portland, and a nice area for an afternoon walk with beautiful views of Casco Bay, is Mackworth Island. This is only about 5 miles from the jetport, again north on Route 295. There is a school for the deaf on Mackworth and a trail that circumnavigates the island, less than 1 mile in total distance. Panoramic views of Casco Bay are your reward for finding this gem of a spot.

In town activities include the Portland Museum of Art, which is on Federal Street, a 5-minute walk from the old port. The museum has a permanent collection that features some Maine artists like Homer and Wyeth. It's a quiet, relaxing place to spend a couple of hours.

If You Go:

Choose Portland, as your destination on a summer day. Prearrange for a courtesy car from Northeast Air and head out for brunch at the Deering Oaks Park, just 3 miles from the field. There is a restaurant here called The Barking Squirrel, and it offers lobster eggs Benedict for a brunch special. This is *the* alternative to low-cholesterol--all cholesterol! It is delicious, though, and reasonably priced at about $6. This is "Down East organic" cooking. The waitstaff are friendly and give new meaning to the concept "laid back." After brunch, head to Freeport for some serious shopping. After you get tired of the crowds and overbearing commercial activity, or have exhausted your credit limit, head out of town to Wolfe's Neck Woods State Park. This is only a few miles to the east from Freeport and has a lovely shoreline to walk. On your way back to Portland, stop in the old port for a drink or just to walk along the waterfront. You can see the lobster boats unloading their catch or watch any of the other local boating activity. There are mail boats and ferries that go out to some of the islands in Casco Bay, and these are well worth exploring in favorable weather. Long Island has a wonderful beach where you can spend a few hours on a sunny afternoon. You can go for a whalewatch cruise as well, if you are in more of the passive tourist mood. Whatever you choose, most activities leave from around the same area at the waterfront in the old port. For some exercise, stop at Mackworth Island and walk the loop or climb around on the rocks at Two Lights State Park.

My favorite restaurants for dinner in Portland are Street & Company (Wharf Street) and Walter's Café (on Exchange Street). Both are moderately priced and offer a mix of Italian fare and seafood.

The Portland area has some beautiful beaches that never get crowded, even in the high summer season. My favorite is Scarborough for scenic beauty, but Old Orchard Beach is best for people-watching and entertaining your kids. It stretches for 10 miles, and the hard sand is perfect for walking. Park your car at Pine Point and walk south along the beach. When you smell the fried dough and see the cotton candy, you'll know you're at the boardwalk. If you like to run on the beach, Pine Point is an excellent place to start from. The fine, hard-packed sand lends itself nicely to a lengthy jog, especially at low tide. Old Orchard Beach is not the French Riviera in terms of sophistication, but it has plenty of character and has been the summer haven for French Canadian families over many years. It's a great place to people-watch, dress down, and just be yourself.

Contacts:
Northeast Air
(207) 774-6318

Portland International Jetport
Portland, 04101

Portland Museum of Art
(207) 773-2787
7 Congress Square
Portland, 04101

Street & Company Restaurant
(207) 775-0007
33 Wharf Street
Portland, 04101

Walter's Café
(207) 871-9258
15 Exchange Street
Portland, 04101

Rangeley (8B0)

Location: North-central Maine

Airfield: The 2700-foot paved strip at Rangeley is not hard to find given its proximity to the lake and to the Rangeley Non-Directional

Beacon (NDB). I have flown the NDB approach here in instrument conditions and can attest to the fact that it is "doable." The airport is bounded by 4000-foot peaks to the southeast but a relatively clear area to the north and west. It is very quiet here, and although the runway is well maintained, summer and winter, help and services can be scarce at times.

Activities:
1. Lake fishing and boating
2. Skiing and snowmobiling
3. Hiking and climbing
4. Off-road cycling

Background: This region of north-central Maine has much to offer year-round. The warm weather brings hikers and backpackers to this area, as the Appalachian Trail cuts through the region of 4000-foot mountains. Camping grounds are not far from the airport, but if you value a shower and a firm bed, hotel accomodations are available in all price ranges as well.

Another favorite activity is fishing. Lake trout as well as salmon anglers flock to the six Rangeley lakes to try their luck during all seasons. The lakes are clean and beautiful and ideal for swimming, too. Boat rental as well as tours and charter fishing are all possible. The wildlife in this region is perhaps second to none in Maine. A friend once told me she wanted to see a moose, and we headed for Rangeley. We were not disappointed, as we saw several coming down to the water at daybreak. Compared to other recreational areas in New England, Rangeley is less commercial, and quite well preserved from an environmental standpoint.

During the autumn, Rangeley hosts a number of hunters, but if hunting is not your sport, it is still an enchanting place to weekend and enjoy the fall foliage.

Winter sports in Rangeley include downhill and cross-country skiing along with snowmobiling. Saddleback Mountain is the local downhill ski area. This mountain is great for a relaxing day with the kids. It rarely gets too crowded. There are many trails for cross-country skiing, and opportunities to experience the serenity and surrounding wildlife are all here. Some, but not all, of the same cross-country ski trails are shared by people snowmobiling, a popular activity among those that frequent the Rangeley area in winter. Ski

Rangeley (8B0)

2500'

MOUNTAINS

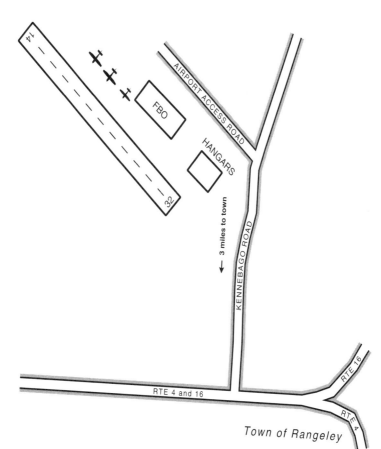

14

FBO

HANGARS

32

AIRPORT ACCESS ROAD

3 miles to town

KENNEBAGO ROAD

RTE 4 and 16

RTE 16

RTE 4

Town of Rangeley

RANGELEY LAKEFRONT

rental, both cross-country and downhill, is readily available and guided snowmobile tours are also possible.

Ice-out and springtime occur rather late here. Often, there is the illusion that winter runs right into summer. Most important, this area is one to avoid during black fly season, usually mid- to late June.

Accommodations range from camping to elegant country bed & breakfasts. The Rangeley Inn is a lakeside motel that offers free transportation to and from the airfield. The rooms are reasonably priced, clean, and comfortable. The staff are helpful in making your stay comfortable, and also in orienting you to the surrounding area. There is a large fireplace with comfortable chairs in the lobby, a perfect place to curl up with a magazine, book, or good friend. The inn organizes activities and offers some great package deals. Understand that there may be a banquet or a reunion on any given weekend; this is a family-type place.

Mallory's B&B Inn is a private lakefront bed & breakfast. This is a great place to spend a couple of days, and your hosts will see to it that you stay busy. The inn offers the use of canoes and boats to guests. Your hosts, Jay and Jane Mallory, will even arrange a seaplane ride for you, if you wish.

Author's Suggestion:

Visit Rangeley in the wintertime and pray for the full cooperation of Mother Nature. Call ahead to check the status of the airport, even if you have checked NOTAMS. Spend a day cross-country skiing or even take a snowmobile guided tour. Choose a bed & breakfast by inquiring at the Rangeley Lakes Tourist Information Service (See Contacts below).

Alternatively, visit Rangeley in late summer. Rent a boat, if you feel adventurous, or take a tour if you want to just sit back and enjoy a lake cruise. Get up early and go for a nature walk and a short hike. Bring your camera so you can show your friends what a moose really looks like! If you want to stay land-based, ask about the Appalachian Trailhead closest to your motel or inn and experience some of this region by foot.

Rangeley has so much to offer that it is hard not to find an activity you will long remember as a unique experience.

Contacts:

The Rangeley Inn and Motor Lodge
    (207) 864-3341 or (800) MOMENTS
    Rangeley, 04970

Rangeley Lakes Region Chamber of Commerce
(207) 864-5364 or (800) MT-LAKES
P.O. Box 317
Rangeley, 04970

Rangeley Airport FBO
(207) 864-5307

Mallory's B&B Inn
(207) 864-2121 or (800) 722-0397 or (207) 864-5316
P.O. Box 9, Hyatt Road
Rangeley, 04970

Gadabout Gaddis (Private)

Location: Gadabout Gaddis Airfield is in Bingham, about 30 miles north of Waterville, in the eastern part of central Maine. Waterville is about 30 miles from the coast.

Airfield: Gadabout Gaddis is a 2000-foot turf runway. The orientation is north-south, and the elevation is 342 feet above sea level. When I visited this place, I was very impressed with how smooth the landing surface is. This is like landing on a golf course fairway. The field runs next to a river at the bottom of a dam, so precision with short-field landings is required. On the other hand, the approach is open and relatively straightforward. I suggest a fly by to look at the windsock on an adjacent building and to plan your approach carefully. The field is somewhat difficult to pick out if you do not know the landmarks. The easiest way to find this place is to follow the 015-degree radial off the Augusta Victor Omni Range (VOR), approximately 50 miles from the VOR station. If you want to intercept this with a Bangor VOR, you'll find it on the 305-degree radial from Bangor.
 The field lies just to the south of a power plant and just to the east of the river below the dam. These landmarks make it relatively easy to find on a clear day. This is a VFR summer airfield. It is listed as private, but is open to the public. Call Jim Ernst at Maine Whitewater for information about field conditions (see Contacts).

Activities:
1. Whitewater rafting

Rafting "The Forks"

2.   Mountain biking.
3.   Hiking

Background: The Forks, Maine, is about 10 miles north of the field. It is here that two rivers, the Kennebec and the Penobscot, come together. This is a well-known spot for the commencement of white-water rafting trips run by several local outfits. Rafting and biking in summer and snowmobiling in winter have influenced the economic rejuvenation of this area. Several inns and bed & breakfasts have sprung up in response to these activities. Each day, a certain volume of water is released from the power stations along the river to create a dramatic surge of white water for rafting and kayaking. Fishermen have river access at either end of the day, morning and evening, while white-water specialists—rafters and kayakers—take to the rapids during the middle of summer days.

If You Go:
Although there are many companies that lead guided tours on this section of the Kennebec and Penobscot, I recommend Northern Outdoors, perhaps the oldest company that leads guided rafting tours. This is a perfect experience to share with a bunch of friends or col-

Gadabout Gaddis

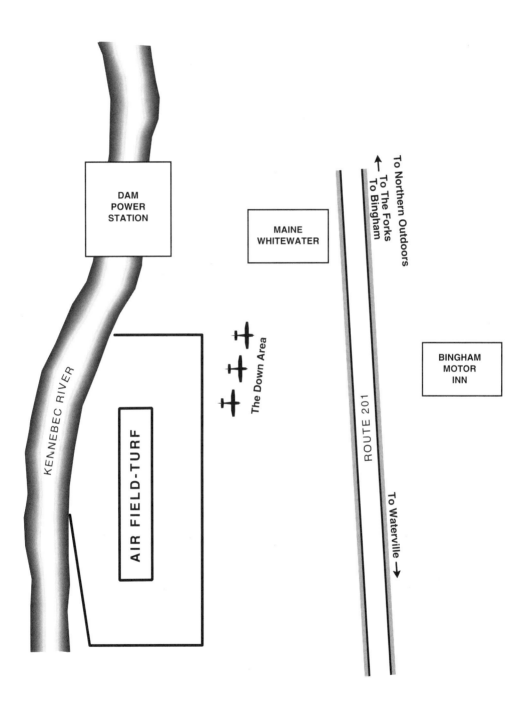

The mighty rafting crew!

leagues. Each of the Northern Outdoors rafts holds from eight to ten people, and this can be a real bonding experience.

Fly with your friends to Gadabout Gaddis and arrange for the people at Northern Outdoors to pick you up there. Northern Outdoors has a headquarters not far from The Forks, where you can relax the evening before your trip at a pub, or even camp, if you wish. Several levels of comfort and accommodations are possible here, from outdoor camping, to sleeping on a cot, to dormitory-style rooms. If you prefer to be away from this somewhat college fraternity-type scene, there are other bed & breakfasts where you could stay nearby.

Each rafting trip starts with a briefing early in the morning on the day of your outing. Plan to be there around 8 A.M. for instructions, breakfast, and a summary of the day's activities. You will not end up hitting the water until 10 A.M., because it takes considerable time for bus transport to the rafting area, wet-suit rental, and equipment familiarization procedures. It is worth renting a wet suit, as the water is quite cool, even on the warmest summer days. For this reason, rafting is more pleasurable at the end of the summer, August or early September, when the water temperature is at its warmest. If you have a full suit, you will be more comfortable and enjoy the experience more. You will get wet, you can count on it. A single day rafting trip gives you more than just a taste of what this sport is all about, so you may want to stop at that. However, overnight trips are available as well.

If you want to stay landlocked, mountain biking excursions are led by the same outfit or by Maine Whitewater, located adjacent to the airfield. The guided tour is quite nice in this area, as the trails are often not well marked and distances between towns are great. This is one of the few places I have been in the Northeast where you get the feeling of going into the backcountry. Bikes and equipment can be rented from the resort center at Northern Outdoors or from Maine Whitewater.

In summary, Gadabout Gaddis is a unique adventure that few pilots I know have experienced. And if you try rafting, it is bound to be an especially memorable adventure at that!

Contacts:

Northern Outdoors Inc.
    (207) 663-4466 or (800) 765-7238
    P.O. Box 100
    The Forks, 04985

Maine Whitewater (Jim Ernst)
    (800) 345-6246

Gadabout Gaddis Airport
    (207) 672-4814
    Bingham, 04920

Riverside Lodge
    (207) 672-3215
    Bingham, 04920

Sugarloaf Airport (B21)

Location: North central Maine, mountainous terrain

Airfield: Sugarloaf Airfield is one of the most difficult and danger-ous places I have ever approached for landing. This is not an attempt to scare the experienced pilot, but rather a warning to the aviator who is unfamiliar with mountain flying and difficult approaches. The 3000-foot paved strip sits in a valley amid 6000-foot peaks. The field is surrounded by trees, and gusty winds are the rule, rather than the exception, here. There is no instrument approach into this airport, so pick your days to fly here with caution and conservatism.

Activities:
1. Golf
2. Skiing (both cross-country and downhill)
3. Fishing
4. Hiking

Background: This is one of the few destination airfields for excellent downhill skiing. Sugarloaf Mountain is just a few miles from the airport, and ground transportation is available and free. If you are staying at the Sugarloaf Mountain Resort, a special courtesy car will fetch you. If you want to come just for the day, the Sugarloaf Mountain Association has a scheduled bus route that stops by the airport. Either way is reliable access to the mountain area. Sugarloaf Mountain has trails that are comparable to almost any other area in the Northeast in terms of difficulty, elevation, and varied terrain. Overcrowding is seldom a problem here, because the area is far enough from any major city. This tends to keep "day-trippers" away. The area at the base of the mountain is less developed than other major ski areas, but still offers a variety of accommodations and restaurants. The cross-country trails are less extensive than Sunday River Resort, for example, but are nevertheless adequate for this type of activity.

Summer activities at Sugarloaf include a challenging golf course as well as mountain biking, hiking, and walking. The golf course, open to the public, is very long and narrow, typical of a mountainside course. The entrance is on the mountain access road, which makes transportation to both the mountain and the golf course easy, free, and convenient.

There is no town of Sugarloaf, only the base lodge area, and the nearest small village is Stratton. The problem with venturing into the area surrounding Sugarloaf Airport is mainly one of transportation. This is a mountainous area and cycling is for the physically fit and you must bring your own bike. Moreover, taxi service is not available and renting a car is next to impossible, despite what the AOPA guide indicates.

The Belgrade Lakes Region, offers some excellent fishing in these parts. In several cases, you can arrange to stay at a resort where the emphasis is on outdoor living with elegantly rustic accommodations. (See suggestions below.)

Sugarloaf (B21)

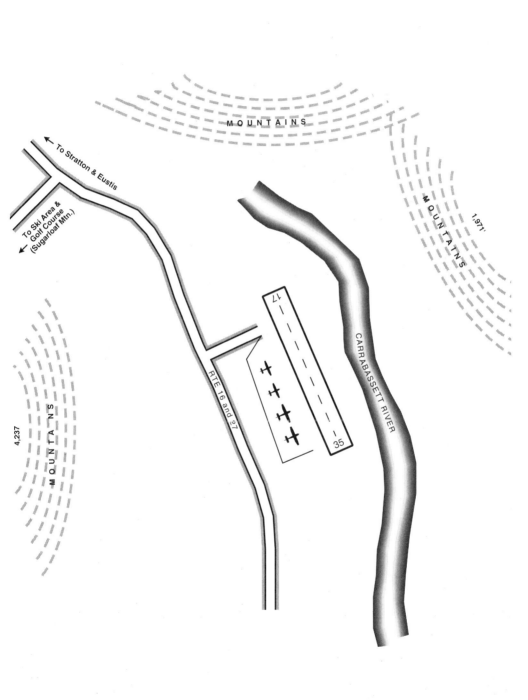

To Stratton & Eustis

To Ski Area &
Golf Course
(Sugarloaf Mtn.)

MOUNTAINS

MOUNTAINS

MOUNTAINS

1,971'

4,237

RTE 16 and 27

CARRABASSETT RIVER

17

35

If You Go:

Winter: Pick a clear calm day in March and fly into Sugarloaf early in the morning. (First call the Sugarloaf bus service and make sure that it is running on this day.) Take the shuttle up to the mountain and enjoy a wonderful day of spring skiing. Catch the bus back to the airport or stay overnight at the Sugarloaf Mountain Inn Resort. They will provide transportation for guests. Another precautionary bit of advice is to leave in the afternoon, when the temperatures are warm enough so that you do not need a preheat, if this applies to your aircraft. There are no services at the airfield for this.

Summer: Fly into Sugarloaf early in the morning, when the winds are light. Stay at Tea Pond Camps, a rustic resort with log cabins on a beautiful lake. It feels like camping, but you sleep well and can shower! The camps are on Tea Pond Road off Tim Pond Road, just on the other side of Eustis Village. Having called ahead, the people at Tea Pond will give you a ride, if you are staying overnight. Enjoy a leisurely day or two at the lake, and partake of home-cooked meals at very reasonable rates. Activities here include hiking, fishing, hunting, and swimming, but most important, a guaranteed peaceful state of mind.

Finally, if you are geared up for an afternoon of frustration and the management of adversity on grass, book a tee time at the Sugarloaf Golf Course. The shuttle bus is your free transportation for this outing.

Contacts:

The general Sugarloaf Mountain area number for accommodations and information is (800) 843-5623.

Sugarloaf Shuttle Bus
    (207) 628-2877

Sugarloaf USA Inn and Condominiums (at the mountain)
    (207) 237-2000
    Carrabassett Valley, 04947

Tea Pond Camps
    (207) 243-2943
    P. O. Box 349
    Stratton, 04982
    Hosts Shelly and Eddie Bear

Bethel (0B1)

Location: Central Maine, near Sunday River Ski Resort

Airfield: Bethel is a short, paved strip that is a relatively easy VFR approach. The region is mountainous, but the approach is fairly clear from the South. There are no facilities at the field, and the runway is not lighted.

Activities:
1. Golf
2. Mountain biking
3. Hiking
4. Skiing (cross-country and downhill)

Background: Bethel, is known to travelers for a number of points of interest. First is the nearby ski area of Sunday River. This resort area has grown over the past several years and now it is the largest ski area in Maine-perhaps even in New England. Crowds are moderate on weekends during the winter, especially on Sunday. The terrain is challenging for eastern skiing, and the area is extensive with respect to number of trails and high-speed lifts. A variety of accommodations including condominiums, hotels, and country inns, are available. The Mountain Corporation has developed a mountain biking center to promote summer activity. This is perhaps one of the most extensive mountain biking areas in all of New England.

The town of Bethel has retained a great deal of its traditional charm, despite the development of the nearby ski area. This is the home of Gould Academy, a private New England preparatory school. Also in town you will find the Bethel Inn. This is a terrific weekend spot for the golfer or for anyone else who wants to separate himself from the activities of the Sunday River area. The golf course is beautiful and challenging. The food at the inn is excellent as well. Several package deals are available for the weekend traveler.

If You Go:
Make plans to stay at the Bethel Inn and call ahead for a brochure of the upcoming activities at the time you will be there. Enjoy a day of golf, hiking, or mountain biking at Sunday River. You can rent all the

Bethel (0B1)

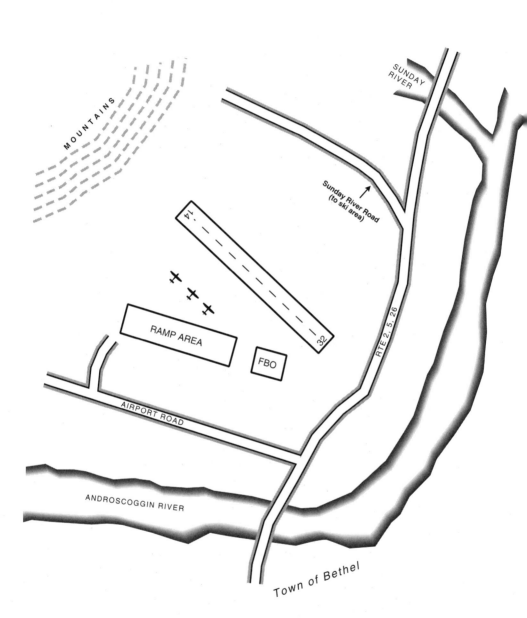

equipment when you arrive. The folks at the inn will help you with these arrangements.

Contacts:
Bethel Inn, and Country Club
     (207) 824-2175
     Bethel, 04217
Sunday River Ski Area
     (207) 824-3000
     Bethel, 04217

Millinocket (MLT)

Location: Millinocket, is in central Maine approximately 10 miles from Mount Katahdin, the highest peak in the state.

Airfield: Millinocket Municipal Airport is located a mile out of town and has two 4000-foot intersecting runways. Instrument approaches, precision and nonprecision, are available. The field is easily visible with wide open spaces. This is a good practice field for the student pilot.

Activities:
1. Hiking
2. Climbing
3. White water rafting
4. Canoeing
5. Float plane trips
6. Fishing
7. Mountain biking

Background: For the outdoorsman, a trip to Millinocket is really a trip to the Katahdin Mountain area. Katahdin is the highest peak in Maine and is surrounded by an abundance of beautiful streams and lakes. You could spend many days here and not run out of things to do.

The local FBO at Millinocket Municipal is typically Maine. The people are helpful, humble, and move at their own pace. It's possible to rent a car at the field, but don't expect a luxury vehicle. In fact, the last time I rented one, I'm quite sure it wouldn't have passed inspection in most states! Nevertheless, if your objective is to get

Nearly to the top of Mt. Katahdin.

from point A to point B, it will suffice. Be sure to call ahead for a car, because there are only two and one may be in the repair shop, as was the case for me on two occasions.

There is not much to see in the town of Millinocket, but 10 miles north is the entrance to Baxter State Park, where you will find some of the finest climbing, hiking, fishing, and camping in central Maine.

Mount Katahdin is a vigorous climb. I have climbed to the peak several times on different trails. If you plan to climb to the top, you have to start early, be in good physical condition, and wear appropriate clothing, even in the middle of summer. If you are an experienced climber or hiker, do not let me scare you. This is a wonderful adventure, taking about 5 hours for the ascent and about 3 1/2-hours to descend. Different trails afford different degrees of difficulty and danger. The views are spectacular, and on a summer day you will have plenty of company, although it never gets annoyingly crowded. This is Maine, one of America's last frontiers. Katahdin is the very end (or the beginning) of the Appalachian Trail. You may run into someone who is starting out on a three-month hike or someone who is finishing one. The latter group of hikers have a very distinct odor and plenty of stories. Even if it is a beautiful day, bring some over-clothes. One day, I was climbing and the temperature at the bottom

Millinocket (MLT)

was 75 degrees. We measured 40 degrees at the summit. Camping at Katahdin is very popular. Weekend reservations are a must, and an Appalachian Trail map is useful as well.

Not far from the entrance of Baxter State Park is the Big Moose Inn. This is a rustic, country inn located about 8 miles outside of Millinocket on the way to the park entrance. There is a restaurant at the inn that features good home cooking. This place has a tremendous amount of character, as the floors are all crooked and the mantels are filled with mounted animals and prized game fish. The innkeepers are friendly, helpful, and native to the area. Across the street, you can start out on a rafting trip down the Penobscot River. Different-length trips are available and reservations are required. If you desire a more relaxing day or weekend, hire a canoe or boat from the lakeshore just adjacent to the Big Moose Inn. Rates are reasonable, and the lake fishing is very good. Float plane service with guided fishing trips is available. Native brook trout are indigenous to some of the more remote lakes and are the main objective to these outings.

If You Go:

Reserve a car from the Millinocket Municipal Airport; preferably, do not take the station wagon! Stay at the Big Moose Inn and get up early. Read about the different trails at the entrance to Baxter State Park, where information booklets are available. The Knife Edge is notorious for being the most difficult and technical hike. My favorite is the Katahdin Stream Trail, which offers a wide variety of terrain and views. As the name implies, it winds next to a stream at the lower elevations. The last third of the hike is the most difficult and time-consuming. Although no ropes or special equipment are required, at several spots you must hoist yourself up over a ledge or slide on your seat over boulders. Even if you do not make this last part, you are guaranteed to be satisfied with commanding views of the surrounding ranges.

My second choice is a single-day rafting expedition with the Northern Outdoors Company. This is a great experience, especially with a group of your friends. The best time of year for this is at the end of summer, when the water is warm enough so that you do not mind being splashed or plunging over the side of the boat between courses of rapids. Unless it is an extremely warm day, bring a wet suit or rent one. You will be in the boat for a long afternoon, and if you get chilled, it is hard to warm up. This is a wonderful experience, especially for the first-time rafter.

Contacts:
Baxter State Park (Mount Katahdin area)
    (207) 723-5140
    Park Headquarters, 64 Balsam Drive
    Millinocket, 04462

Plain Air (FBO and Rental Car)
    (207) 723-6649

Northern Outdoors Rafting
    (800) 765-7238
    Millinocket Airport, 04462

Big Moose Inn
    (207) 723-8391
    Millinocket Lake
    Millinocket, 04462

Katahdin Air Service (Float Plane Service)
    (207) 723-8378
    P.O. Box 171
    Millinocket, 04462

Appalachian Trail Conference
    (304) 535-6331
    P.O. Box 807
    Harpers Ferry, WV 25425

MASSACHUSETTS

Plum Island (2B2)

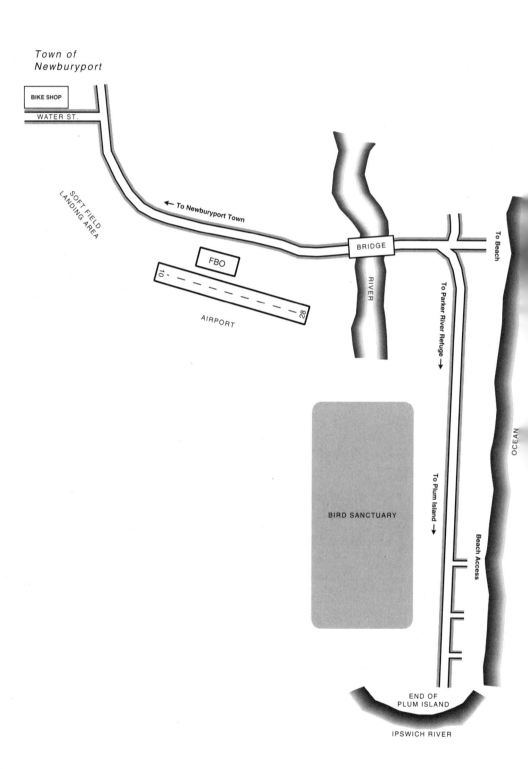

Plum Island (2B2)

Location: Plum Island airport is one mile from the town of Newbury-port on the north shore of Massachusetts approximately 30 miles from Boston.

Airfield: This is a 2500-foot paved runway, with a relatively rough paved surface. It can be challenging to land at. A nonprecision instrument approach is available. The approach to runway 28, over the water and wetlands, is more open, with no obstructions or trees. On the other hand, I have experienced significant ground effect when trying to land from this direction. The opposite direction, heading east, involves coming in over trees onto a relatively short field. Either way, you have to be precise in hitting the numbers, depending on the ground roll you require.

The local FBO is small with sparse amenities and limited hours of attendance. Call ahead if you think you are going to need assistance. A few ultralight pilots are usually around and can be helpful.

Activities:
1. Bird-watching at the Parker River Wildlife Refuge
2. Cycling (rental shop about a half-mile walk)
3. Beach (a 1-mile walk)
4. Excellent restaurants in town
5. Antiquing

Background: Plum Island is a wonderful spot to spend a summer afternoon. The airport lies approximately 1 mile from the historic town of Newburyport, a typical New England coastal village. In town you can browse antique's shops, visit art galleries, and enjoy gourmet food stores. This is a fine place for brunch, lunch, or even dinner. Restaurants can be found in all price ranges and levels of formality. The town is quaint and its New England charm has been preserved. There are several first-rate bed & breakfasts for the overnight visitor.

Traveling east and away from town, on the main road from the airport, you will find Plum Island's wildlife refuge. This is run by the Trustees of Reservations, an organization committed to the preservation of lands and wildlife in Massachusetts. It costs $5 to travel on the refuge by car and $2 for pedestrians and cyclists, although the gate is not always monitored. The 7-mile access road leads through an abundance of marshland, which is prime habitat for birds. On a weekend day, you will find birdwatchers lined up with their telescopes and binoculars in field dress. Along the road, there is beach access. Even on the most beautiful of summer days, it never gets crowded here. There are 7 miles of beachfront. Bring your own refreshments, though, because there is no commercial activity along this beach. This same road is ideal for a bicycle trip with the family. Cars move slowly and courteously along the road, which is wide enough for both types of vehicles. Bring or rent a bicycle capable of varied terrain. While the surface does not qualify as trail riding, it is a bit too rugged for the average 10-speed. A hybrid model bicycle would do fine, though, and these can be rented just outside the town of Newburyport.

If You Go:

Fly into Newburyport on a summer morning and walk half a mile toward town. Ask someone where Middle Street Foods is, in town. This is a sandwich place with an organic influence! The soups and specials are excellent and leave some room for dessert.

Next, either browse through town or head out to the refuge by bicycle. Bikes can be rented at the Riverside Bike Shop, which is on Water Street in Newburyport. Rent the bicycles for at least 2 hours and ride out onto Plum Island. This route will take you back past the airport, so you can leave any towels or beachwear in the plane and retrieve them on your way to the beach. The bicycle store closes around 6 P.M., so plan your day accordingly. You do not have to travel the full 7 miles to the very tip of the island, for the beach is beautiful all along the way. Cycle until you get a flavor for the area and then choose a convenient marked path down to the water through the dunes. There are plenty of signs and explanations for beach access. Taxi service is available from the airfield or from Newburyport, if you prefer not to bicycle.

Contacts:

Parker River National Wildlife Refuge
   (978) 465-5753

Air Plum Island (FBO)
   (978) 462-2144

Taxi
   (978) 465-2333

Riverside Bike Shop

(978) 465-5566

Greater Newburyport Chamber of Commerce
(978) 462-6680
29 State Street
Newburyport, 01950

Beverly (BVY)

Location: North shore of Massachusetts

Airfield: Beverly Airport has three well-maintained paved runways of sufficient width and length to facilitate an easy landing in most crosswind conditions. It is a great place to practice nonprecision approaches, as there is no Instrument Landing System (ILS) here. The surrounding area is free of obstacles, and the traffic is usually very light, perhaps too light to justify a control tower. Nevertheless, the tower continues to function and the field continues to provide good services to general aviation pilots. There are two sides to the Beverly Airport, east and west, and the field is split down the middle between two towns. Half of Beverly Airport is actually in the town of Danvers. As such, one of the entrances to the field, by car, is in Danvers and the other is in Beverly. (see map for details.) Both sides offer fuel, flight instruction, and pilot accessories at separate FBOs.

Activities:
1. Museums
2. Walking
3. Hiking

Background: Beverly Airport is situated approximately 4 miles from the coastal town of Beverly and approximately 6 miles from downtown Salem. While this is not a well-known resort area, there are several possibilities for an interesting day or weekend trip.

If you are looking for a good place to stretch your legs, perhaps to refuel and take an hour's break, this is an excellent spot. Across from the Beverly-side entrance of the airport is an area owned by the Audobon Society of Massachusetts. Here is a network of wooded walking paths and trails that wind around the west side of Lake

Beverly (BVY)

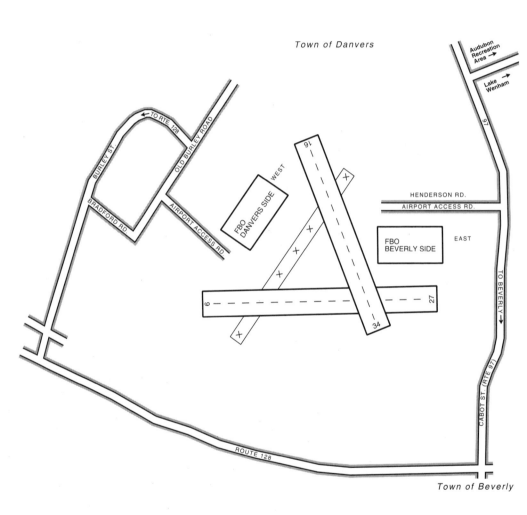

Wenham. The trails are clearly marked and perfect for an hour or two of stress relief and exercise. The surroundings are calm, and you are unlikely to see anyone else here.

A taxi ride into Beverly is about $7. Here you will find a quiet coastal town with several good restaurants and, on Sunday afternoon, a special treat for your children. Le Grand David is a magic act, that has been performed in Beverly for many years. The show takes place in an old-fashioned theater, the Cabot Street Cinema, which is the perfect setting. The magic show is appropriate for all ages-adults are seldom disappointed with the performance. A number of excellent restaurants are within walking distance of the theater. Across Cabot Street is a fine Italian restaurant called Chianti. This small eatery is dimly lit, quiet, and elegant, featuring northern Italian cuisine. The food complements its ambience, yet the price is fairly reasonable. For something less formal, but equally as close, about 15 yards across a side street from the theater is a place called Tappas Corner. This sandwich shop features ethnic foods with an organic flair. If you can find a seat, this is an excellent pre- or post-performance stop.

The town of Salem neighbors Beverly, and is of great historic significance. Several museums and points of interest are worth visiting, particularly if you are a student of the history of witchcraft. The historic district is a great place to stroll and take in some of the architecture. There are a number of interesting boutiques for shopping as well.

If You Go:

Plan a trip to Beverly Airport during the fall season on a Sunday. Take a taxi to the Cabot Street Cinema and see Le Grand David Magic Show with your children. Have a bite to eat before or after at Tappas Corner or at Chianti (reservations suggested).

Halloween is perhaps the busiest time of year in Salem and a great time to visit. Head into town for a lesson in history at the Salem Witch Museum or at the House of Seven Gables. Walk around the waterfront and stop in at The Pig's Eye for some great pub food with a Mexican flavor. Visit the Hawthorne Hotel for a more formal and old-style New England atmosphere. This place is also nice for a quiet weekend with someone special.

Contacts:

Beverly Airport FBO (Beverly Flight Center)
    (978) 774-7755
Hawthorne Hotel (Salem)

(978) 744-4080 or (800) 7297829
18 Washington Square West
Salem, 01970

Le Grand David Magic Show (Cabot Street Cinema)
(978) 927-3677
268 Cabot Street
Beverly, 01915

Chianti Restaurant (Beverly)
(978) 921-2233
285 D. Cabot Street
Beverly, 01915

Salem Witch Museum
(978) 744-1692
19 1/2 Washington Square North
Salem, 01970

The House of Seven Gables Museum (Salem)
(978) 744-0091
54 Turner Street
Salem, 01970

The Pig's Eye Restaurant (Salem)
(978) 741-4436
148 Derby Street
Salem, 01970

Salem Chamber of Commerce
(978) 744-0004
Old Town Hall, 32 Derby Square
Salem, 01970

Hanscom Field, Bedford (BED)

Location: Ten miles north of Boston, in Bedford

Airfield: Hanscom Field is one of the general aviation gateways to
the Boston metropolitan area. This large airport, with three intersecting runways and multiple instrument approaches, is shared by
civilian and military air traffic. There is a large military base adjacent
to the field, but the military aviation traffic is not particularly heavy.

On the other hand, the civilian air traffic can provide for a frustrating delay during heavy periods of use. Despite the "big-city" atmosphere, Hanscom is easy enough for the inexperienced GA pilot, and I would not hesitate to recommend it as such.

Activities:
1. Cycling
2. Museums
3. Historic New England towns
4. Bird-watching

Background: Virtually all members of the New England aviation community are familiar with Hanscom Field. The surrounding area, however, has some unique activities to offer, which you may not be aware of. In addition, this is the only airport, with the exception of Logan International, that offers public transportation into the city of Boston.

For the cycling enthusiast, the Minuteman Trail passes right by Hanscom Field. Access to the trail, a 12-mile-long paved and protected bike path, is less than a mile from the military entrance to the field. The path leads from Bedford to Cambridge, terminating at the end of one of Boston's high-speed subway routes, the Red Line. The trail is smooth-surfaced and ideal for cycling and/or in-line skating. Numerous facilities to rest, drink, or snack are available along the path. On weekends and summer evenings, it gets quite crowded as pedestrians and joggers use it, too. Nevertheless, people seem to obey the rules of the road, and very few accidents occur.

Just adjacent to Hanscom Field off Route 2A is the Minuteman National Park. This area has great historical significance from Revolutionary War times and is a lovely place for a walk. There are written explanations along the trail and periodically guided tours are available as well, leaving from a small information center about half a mile from the entrance to Hanscom Field, east on Route 2A.

Not far from Hanscom, in Lincoln, is the DeCordova Museum, an open-air sculpture park combined with an indoor gallery. The collection is unique in its promotion of renowned New England contemporary artists. During the summer, there are occasional afternoon concerts, and an outdoor café completes this culturally rich experience.

Another activity, that is popular around this area is bird-watching. The Great Meadows Nature Preserve along the Concord River is just a few minutes from Hanscom by car. This area of marshland is

Hanscom Field, Bedford (BED)

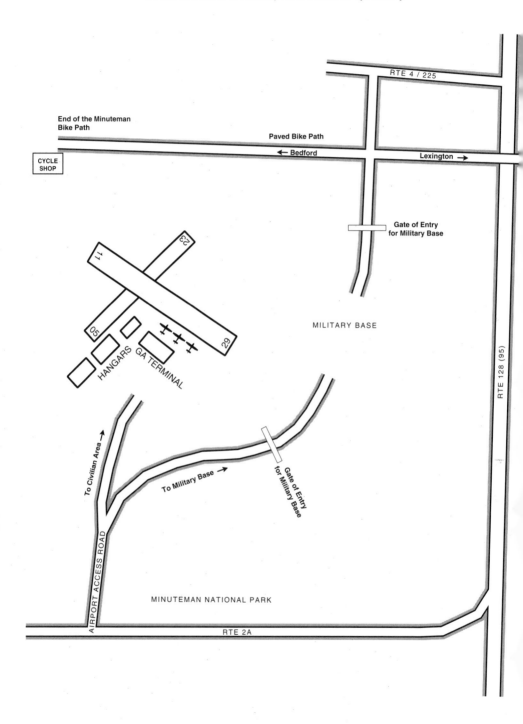

particularly well known to serious birders, and you'll see these folks out in full regalia at various times.

For the rough and general layout of these activities, see the map illustrating their relationship to Hanscom Field.

Transportation from Hanscom offers a couple of options. First, if you are headed into Boston and want to use public transportation, you can arrive in the central city without much difficulty. With the exception of Sundays, a bus leaves from the airport connecting with the high-speed subway, the Red Line. The Red Line will take you from Alewife Station to Harvard Square or all the way into the central city, Park Street Station. At Park Street, you can connect with virtually all lines branching out around suburban Boston. If you prefer to drive yourself, major car rental agencies are available from Hanscom Field.

If You Go:
Choose a summer day for your trip to Hanscom Field. Bring your own bicycles or call ahead to the Bikeway Source Cycle Shop, located on one end of the Minuteman Trail. Here you can rent bicycles, but you will have to take a 4-mile cab ride to get them. Head to the Minuteman Trail, just adjacent to Hanscom Field (see map). Cycle along the Minuteman Trail from Bedford toward Arlington and Cambridge. At the end of the trail (12 miles total), lock your bicycles at Alewife Station and take the subway to Harvard Square. Take a walk around Harvard Square, through Harvard Yard, or along the Charles River. If you are in the mood for relaxing, just hang out and watch the street shows and interesting people. There are plenty of restaurants for lunch or dinner, ranging from the most casual in atmosphere to elegantly sophisticated bistros. During summer evenings, street performers provide free entertainment (or at least they thrive on donations from a sympathetic crowd).

If you have never been to this part of Massachusetts, you may want to explore the area around Hanscom Field. Minuteman National Park is an interesting historical feature for children and adults alike. The Lexington Chamber of Commerce will send you a wealth of information pertaining to the history of this region. I suggest stopping for lunch in the town of Concord. The Colonial Inn has a great pub for sandwiches and drinks for anyone but the left-seat occupant!

If the weather is cooperative, visit the grounds of the DeCordova Museum. Walk the grounds of the sculpture park and then daydream amid this meadow of contemporary work from your seat at the café.

Contacts:

The Bikeway Source Cycle Shop
    (781) 275-7799
    111 South Road
    Bedford, 01730

The Colonial Inn
    (978) 369-9200
    48 Monument Square
    Concord, 01742

The DeCordova Museum and Scupture Park
    (781) 259-3604
    51 Sandy Pond Road
    Lincoln, 01773

Lexington Chamber of Commerce
    (781) 862-2480

Executive Flyers Aviation
    (617) 274-7227 (one of the many FBOs at Hanscom Field)

Chatham (CQX)

Location: Cape Cod, Massachusetts (mid-Cape)

Airfield: Chatham is an uncontrolled airport with a nonprecision instrument approach. The visual approach is easy and free of unexpected hazards. The folks at the local FBO are quite helpful, kind, and extremely hospitable. This seems to be a popular hangout for several of the veteran GA pilots indigenous to the area. They are valuable resources for directions, advice, and accounts of their own flying adventures. A few times, these kind folks have offered me a lift into town without my asking.

While Chatham is not the busiest airport on the Cape or islands by any means, the common traffic advisory frequency and the Unicom frequency are shared by many other of the local VFR uncontrolled airports in this region. This makes communications difficult, if not impossible, at high use times. The best suggestion I can offer is to broadcast your intentions clearly, have patience, and use as little

Chatham FBO, Photo by L. K. Pickett.

technical jargon as possible.

Activities:
1. Beach activities
2. Golf
3. Boating
4. Sight-seeing on Cape Cod, Massachusetts

Background: Chatham, a community on Cape Cod, has not changed much over the past 20 years. Its clean, quiet, and traditionally "Cape" atmosphere makes it a popular spot for honeymooners and a quieter weekending crowd. The town is full of antique shops and tasteful boutiques, as well as a few restaurants and sandwich shops. The beachfront is unspoiled, and Monomoy Island, a national wildlife refuge, stretches 10 miles toward the south just across from the main public beach. This haven for wildlife, waterfowl, and other animals is a long, sandy spit, that can provide you with hours of beach walking, reflection, and solitude. In the winter months, the island is inhabited by birds and seals. If you are at all interested, I suggest a flyby over the area to survey the island. One time I did this, and I was truly impressed by the number and variety of seals on the

Chatham (CQX)

shoreline. There were thousands of these creatures, creating the illusion of a rocky shore. This is another benefit of being a GA pilot.

If you are looking for a quiet weekend escape, there are many bed & breakfasts in the area and a couple of resort accommodations as well. Many of these are open in the off-season and offer great discounts and package deals to entice you there at this time. The Cape is becoming increasingly accustomed to winter tourism and, as such, more and more small businesses remain open in the off-season, especially on weekends. If you can bear the blustery weather, it is a great getaway.

If You Go:
Try exploring this part of the Cape in the fall. Bring plenty of warm clothing and take someone special to the Chatham Bars Inn. This is a popular, large resort just adjacent to the beach and not far from town. The resort has planned activities, especially on weekends, and can help you make the most of your time here. They will send you literature on the resort as well as the surrounding area to help spark your interest and plan your activities. The Bars Inn is frequented by people who return each year to this special place. There is golf adjacent to the resort, but it is by no means a championship course. My favorite activity here is a long walk on Monomoy Island complete with picnic lunch, weather permitting. Unless you know someone with a boat, you will have to arrange for transportation to this place, and this can be done by taking the "water taxi" from the fish pier at Chatham Harbor. This service is available only in the summer and early fall.

In the evening, try the main dining room at the Bars Inn. This is elegant and somewhat pricey, but in this case you get what you pay for!

Contacts:
FBO at Chatham Airport
    (508) 945-9000

Chatham Bars Inn
    (508) 945-0096 or (800) 527-4884
    Share Road
    Chatham, 02633

Taxi service at Chatham

(508) 945-0068

Car rental at Chatham
    (508) 945-0242

Chatham Chamber of Commerce
    (508) 430-7455 or (800) 715-5567

Bert & Carol's Lawnmower and Bicycle Shop
    (508) 945-0137
    347 Route 28
    North Chatham

Monomoy Island Ferry
    (508) 945-5450
    P.O. Box 38
    West Chatham, 02669

Monomoy Island Information
    (508) 945-0096

Provincetown (PVC)

Location: Provincetown, or Race Point Airfield, sits at the very tip of Cape Cod

Airfield: Race Point is an area of beach and conservation land, which is just adjacent to the landing strip. There is heavy use of the airfield in the summer, with quite a bit of commercial and recreational activity. In winter, the field is very quiet and attended during daylight hours only. There are two precautions I would advise to the general aviation pilot in planning an approach to Provincetown Municipal Airport during the summer. The first is to be prepared for the use of the extremely busy Unicom frequency. A "heads-up" approach is required on a summer weekend day. The second is that Provincetown is surrounded by the most beautiful dunes on the Cape. These undulating mounds of sand that line the shore create pretty significant ground effect, wind shear, and turbulence for the final leg of your approach to runway 25 especially. Be prepared for this, and it will not surprise or unnerve you. Brief your passengers, and you will prepare them for a few seconds of anxiety prior to touchdown. Other than that, the field is easily approached and user-friendly. There is a courtesy golf cart, if you are carrying a lot of beach equipment and need

The shoreline and museum just across the way from Provincetown airport.

a ride to the main terminal area. Taxis are always waiting during the peak season and major rental car agencies are airport-based as well.

Activities:
1. Beach activities
2. Whale watching
3. Cycling and in-line skating
4. Fishing
5. Ocean swimming

Background: There is so much to do in Provincetown and the surrounding area that if you have not yet been here it is time to go. I will start with the natural beauty of this place and then move on to its year-round and summer community activities.

Provincetown is situated at the very end of Cape Cod, and as such you are lucky to be able to fly there in avoiding what could be the worst weekend Cape traffic imaginable. In most small single engine aircraft, the flight would take approximately 30 minutes from Boston, while the drive would be in the neighborhood of 3 hours. There is a paved trail, which runs right by the airport entrance. This

A local fisherman at Provincetown.

turns into a network of protected paths weaving through an area known as the Province Lands. This area reminds me of "Land of the Lost," with its small, contorted shrubs and wind-bent beach grass amid a vast array of dunes, 20 to 30 feet high. The paved path is perfect for bicycles, but there are quite a few steep hills and sharp turns, so exercise caution and wear a helmet. Several signs mark the way into town from these paths. The park rangers discourage in-line skating in the summer, but I have skated here many times during the off-season, when the traffic is light, and the surface is certainly smooth enough. Beware, though, as you come through wooded areas. Pine needles, sand and leaves will blanket the trail, making it treacherous, particularly for in-line skates. The trails wind through the Race Point area, paralleling the main roads in a few places, but remain approximately 1 mile from town. The paths are shared by runners, walkers, cyclists (and the occasional deviant in-line skater), but I have been here in all seasons and never found it too crowded.

The beach at Race Point is beautiful, and there is enough of it that privacy is virtually guaranteed if you are willing to walk just a short distance from the main access point. The water is usually fine for swimming. While the waves are not terribly big, the current here is strong . Race Point is famous for striped bass fishing, and you

Provincetown (PVC)

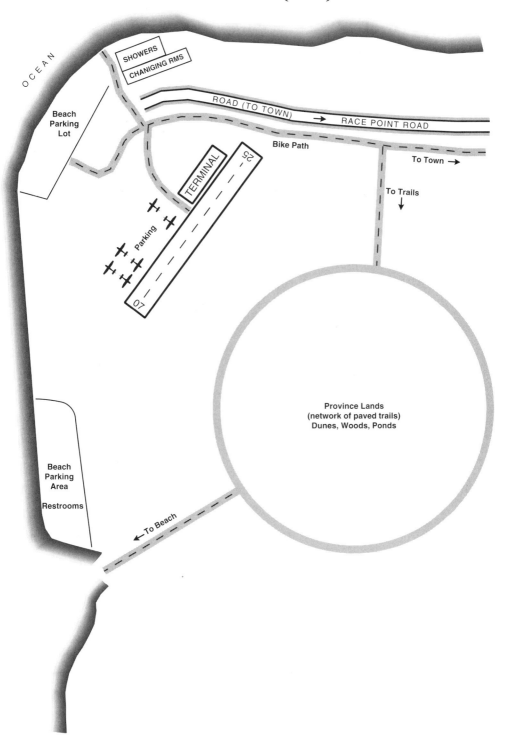

will see recreational vehicles as well as boats in pursuit of bluefish and stripers. I once watched a surf fisherman land a striper here in excess of 40 pounds.

There are no restaurants or snack bars out at Race Point, so picnic lunches must be complete. There are men's and women's communal changing rooms and bathrooms, complete with cold shower, at the beachfront entrance.

As previously mentioned, ground transportation into town is available. A cab ride into town costs about $10 and availability is seldom a problem. You can rent a car, but unless you want to see the surrounding area or tour this part of the Cape, everything in town is within walking distance. There are several inns to stay at, both on the main street, and on quiet side streets. The best way to choose one is by walking around, by stopping at the chamber of commerce, or by recommendation from a friend who has stayed at one of these bed & breakfasts or inns. The turnover rate of small inns is quite high. In fact, the place I stayed at when I was last in Provincetown has changed both ownership and image. For this reason, I am reluctant to make specific recommendations.

Provincetown has the distinction of being a center for alternative lifestyles. Both the gay and lesbian communities have a strong presence here, and it has become a popular spot for the weekend traveler with this focus. There is an avant garde emphasis to this coastal New England town because of its progressive and alternative influences. Numerous galleries, eclectic restaurants, and novelty shops can be found here. Despite its unique identity, though, Provincetown is still very much Cape Cod. There is a lot of tradition and history here, as well as preservation of architecture typical to the region. In town, you will find Portuguese restaurants and bakeries, a local favorite interest of mine.

If You Go:

For a fabulous beach day, choose Provincetown in midsummer. Pack a picnic lunch and bring a luggage valet so that you can wheel your cooler to the beach. Take an ocean swim and rinse off at the beachfront shower area, free of charge. Walk down to Race Point (to the left) and watch the local fishermen surfcast for striped bass. To the right side (south), there are miles of secluded beachfront, if you are in the mood for privacy.

Take a trip into town by taxi or by bicycle. The distance is about

3 1/2 miles, if you go by way of the Province Lands path. Browse the shops in town and try the Stormy Harbor Restaurant for some Portuguese kale soup. The Stormy Harbor is just around the corner from the main wharf area, where the commercial boats are docked. You will see advertisements for charter fishing, boat tours, and whale-watching. Any of these activities is a great way to spend a hot, sunny afternoon.

If you are in Provincetown for an evening and want to experience some of the local flamboyance, there are several possibilities. One type of show, which is common here, is the female impersonation routine. Several cabaret-style clubs offer this, and you can have dinner while being entertained. You have to have an open mind and also be somewhat willing to be engaged in the whole experience. The entertainers are nonthreatening, but will go out into the audience and mingle and sing. After dinner, there are several outdoor cafés where you can sit and people-watch. This may be the simplest and best entertainment of all.

You will find that Provincetown has very much to offer. There is a New England flavor here, but it's far from a typical New England town in many respects, and worlds apart in others!

Contacts:
Provincetown Chamber of Commerce
    (508) 487-3424
    P.O. Box 1017, 307 Commercial Street
    Provincetown, 02657

Province Lands Visitor Center
    (508) 487-1256

The Stormy Harbor Restaurant
    (508) 487-1680
    277 Commercial Street
    Provincetown, 02657

Taxi service from Provincetown Airport
    (508) 487-3333 or (508) 487-2222
    Race Point Road
    Provincetown, 02657

Budget Rental Car from Provincetown Airport
    (508) 487-4557
    Race Point Road
    Provincetown, 02657

Arnold's Bike Shop

(508) 487-0844
329 Commercial Street
Provincetown, 02657

Provincetown Whale Watch Inc.
(508) 487-3322 or (800) 992-9333
MacMillan Wharf
Provincetown, 02657

Edgartown/Katama Air Park (1B2)

Location: Katama Air Park is located on the southeastern corner of Martha's Vineyard, off the coast of Cape Cod

Airfield: This is a network of turf runways, narrow and unlighted. The longest runway (03-21) is just over 3000 feet and the surface is variable according to season and field conditions. It is one of the easier grass strips to get in and out of, though, with three intersecting runways, although not all may be in use. The runways are narrow with grass on each side, but the approach area is vast and visibility is excellent. Traffic can be heavy, especially on weekends in the summer season. Plenty of parking is available, and there are two parking areas, quite a distance from each other. Be sure to communicate well with Unicom on your approach so that you can specify where you want to park. If you are headed into town, you should park by the FBO, hangar, and restaurant. If you are headed to the beach, there is a special designated area, which is 50 yards from the shoreline. Occasionally, on summer beach days, this lot can be completely full. The FBO attendant is helpful and courteous, but he may be busy, so make your intentions clear. Remember, you cannot leave here after dark, so plan accordingly.

Activities:
1. Beachcombing
2. Cycling
3. In-line skating
4. Surf fishing

Background: Katama Air Park is one of two public airports on Martha's Vineyard. The vineyard had become popular, even before President Clinton began to vacation there but now many people find it trendy and somewhat overbearing during the weekends in high season. Nevertheless, the island offers a tremendous amount of

Katama Air Park at Edgartown has parking near the beach.

beauty, and much attempt has been made to preserve its natural resources. My family has owned a house on Chappaquiddick for many years, and I grew up here in the summer. I have seen the island change, but still find it a special place each time I return.

A trip to Katama does not take much planning, if all you want to do is go to the beach. The adjacent stretch of south beach is nice, and you can walk toward the west to get away from any weekend crowds. Or if you prefer, there is plenty of beach activity and people-watching to the east, by the lifeguard stands.

If you are a cyclist, there is a protected bike path, which starts approximately a half mile from the airport. The path is paved and is suitable for in-line skates as well. I would not suggest skating on a busy day, though I have done it. The bicycle path leads into Edgartown, and then continues to Oak Bluffs or Vineyard Haven, two other relatively large towns.

Edgartown has many quaint shops with a beautiful harbor and all sorts of dining possibilities. Accommodations can be found in almost every price range, but if you are planning a visit in summer,

Edgartown/Katama Air Park (1B2)

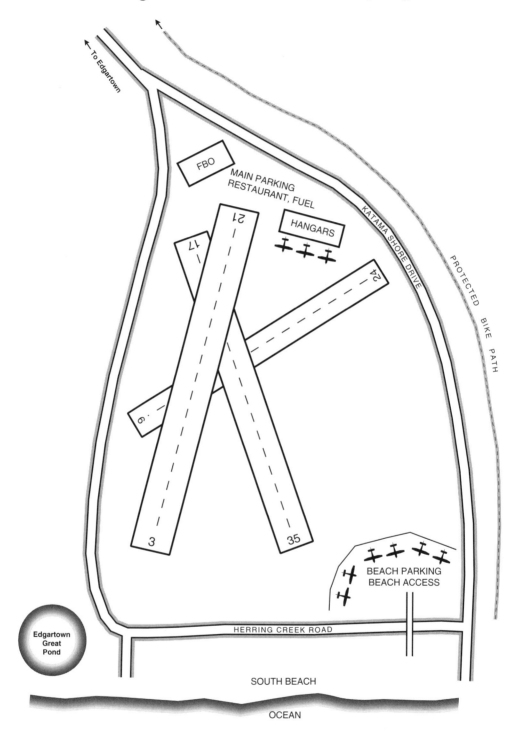

be prepared to pay top dollar. There is a hotel right by the air park, Katama Shores Inn, but this is 2 or 3 miles from Edgartown. Taxi service and shuttle bus service is also available. (See Contacts for details.)

If you are planning a more extensive stay or want to leave in the evening or to rent a car, consider flying to the main airport, Vineyard Haven, in the center of the island.

Martha's Vineyard has so many possibilities as a summer stronghold for activity that you really ought to talk to someone familiar with the island to exploit your specific interests. Give me a call, and I will steer you straight!

If You Go:

Fly to Katama just after Labor Day. Most of the summer crowds will be gone, and the weather is often delightful. Usually the water temperature is perfect for a quick dip, but bring a sweater or fleece top for walking along the beach. If you want warmer water, you can swim in Edgartown Great Pond, approximately 1 1/2 miles to the west of the South Beach access. Take a short walk down the beach, over to the pond, and relax in the warmer water. This is brackish water, as the pond feeds into the ocean for only a short time each spring. Have a picnic on this beach and then head back to your plane at the beach parking area. In the late afternoon, you can go back to the field FBO area to take a warm shower, just to rinse the salt from your skin.

For lunch, have a bite at Mel's Diner at the field, where the food is really good. You may be able to make a contact to get a ride into town. If not, you could take the shuttle or call a taxi for this 3-mile ride. Browse through town, especially the waterfront area and the docks. You will see many people fishing and some beautiful yachts tied up along the wharves. Commercial fishermen bring in striped bass, bluefish, and sharks from time to time. There is plenty of shopping, and a wonderful place to look out over the harbor is just adjacent to the Chappaquiddick Ferry. Climb the stairs to the top of the town dock and sit on the rooftop benches for the best view around.

There are bike shops in town, and you can arrange to ride back to the air park, where you can leave your bicycle for pickup at no extra charge. You cannot, however, pick up the bicycle from the air park. This one-way service is available from most shops, but be sure to ask.

My favorite place for lunch is the pub at The Kelly House, a popular hotel in town. Other overnight accommodations include the Harbor View Hotel, which is quiet, just out of town, close to a beach, and very "Vineyard." Beware, though; it is quite pricey during the summer season. If you are a romantic and have money to burn, you may want to look at the Charlotte Inn. This has a French restaurant on the premises, called L Étoile, which is well known to the discriminating gourmet. The inn is quite elegant and very expensive.

For the cycling enthusiast, a trip to Chappaquiddick is worthwhile. Although there is no protected bike path here, the road is relatively quiet with a smooth surface. Do not be disappointed if you plan on seeing the Dyke Bridge that Edward Kennedy made famous. This structure has been rebuilt twice. Nevertheless, the area at the Dyke Bridge is beautiful and well worth the trip. There is a beach just beyond the bridge, known as East Beach, which is great for swimming and walking. This area of Chappaquiddick lies about approximately 3 1/2 miles from the ferry dock in Edgartown. Ask the ferry captain for easy directions. Watch out for greenhead flies!

Contacts:

Katama Air Park
  (508) 627-9018
  RFD 326
  Edgartown, 02539

John's Taxi
  (508) 627-4677
  Edgartown, 02539

The Kelly House
  (508) 627-7900
  23 Kelley Street
  Edgartown, 02539

Bicycle rental in Edgartown (R.W. Cutler Bike's)
  (508) 627-4052
  1 Main Street
  Edgartown, 02539

Vineyard Haven (MVY)

Location: Vineyard Haven is the main airport on an island 8 miles off the coast of Cape Cod.

Airfield: Vineyard Haven has two intersecting paved runways. The airport features precision and nonprecision instrument approaches and has all the necessary services, including a great little restaurant for breakfast or lunch. The fee for overnight parking is $10 per day. Taxis and rental cars are available. This is an easy place to get in and out of, except on a Friday night, Saturday morning, or Sunday evening during the summer months, when weekend traffic is oppressive. The visual approaches are straightforward and should pose no problems, even to the student pilot.

Activities:
1. Beach activities
2. Cycling
3. In-line skating
4. Sight-seeing

Background: Martha's Vineyard has a different appeal for each person. Of late, it has become somewhat trendy due to its popularity with the First Family. A number of gourmet food stores, expensive art galleries, and posh nightclubs have flourished because of this image. The year-round community of fishermen, farmers, and builders feel differently about the island, though. They recognize their dependency on tourism, and encourage its existence, but some are resentful that the island has become overcrowded during the summer. College students flock here during the summer to work and play at seasonal jobs, and the atmosphere is lively and youthful. Other famous people who have given notoriety to the island include James Taylor, Carly Simon, Walter Cronkite, and Spike Lee. Most of the current celebrities on Martha's Vineyard try to stay out of the public eye and keep a low profile while they are here.

The island is noted for its network of protected bicycle paths. One path begins just outside the airport area and makes a full loop around the airport, mainly through state forestland. This 10-mile loop leads to other paths, which branch out to some of the major towns, notably Vineyard Haven, Oak Bluffs, and Edgartown. You can rent bikes and mopeds at any of the major towns on the Vineyard, the closest to the airport being Oak Bluffs and Edgartown, but not at the airport. Cars and four-wheel-drive vehicles can be rented directly from the airport rental agencies.

Taxi service at Vineyard Haven Airport is convenient, as cabs are always waiting during the summer months. Both shared and private cabs are available.

Across the street from the airport entrance, approximately a quarter of a mile to the west along State Road, is an entrance to one of the most beautiful beaches on the Vineyard. This beach, known as Long Point, is not well marked, and I suspect this is a subconscious effort to preserve its tranquillity and beauty. The land is owned and run by the Trustees of Reservations, an organization dedicated to the preservation of lands and natural wildlife. There is a parking fee for use of this beach, but it is well worth it. The beach is never crowded, even on the most beautiful of days. The surf can be very dangerous, however. The beach closes at 6 P.M., so plan accordingly. The rangers are courteous and helpful, but adamant about clearing the beach at the end of each day. In the off-season, the land is not monitored and access is gained through a different entrance, approximately 2 miles west of the summer entrance. This can be difficult to find, and you may have to try a couple of access roads if you become unsure of where you are. Once you have found the right gate from the main road, the beach is about 2 1/2 miles along a dirt road heading south. Look for the TRUSTEES OF RESERVATIONS sign on the wooden gates. Long Point is a lovely beach, close to the airport, and well worth the effort to find. In the off-season, it is a favorite fishing spot for striped bass and bluefish.

Vineyard Haven Airport is exactly central to the island. The north end of the island is less commercialized and very beautiful. Here you will find the cliffs of Gay Head and the fishing village of Menemsha. Both of these are popular tourist spots, but still not tacky or overpopulated. The middle of the island has some farms and forestlands, while the south end of the island, Chappaquiddick, has beautiful beaches, saltwater ponds, birds, and nature preserves.

Martha's Vineyard has many spots that are unspoiled, yet it has all the amenities of sophisticated travel and accommodation. You can have a splendid picnic or splurge on a gourmet meal. Be sure to ask someone who has been here for specific recommendations in your area of interest.

Vineyard Haven (MVY)

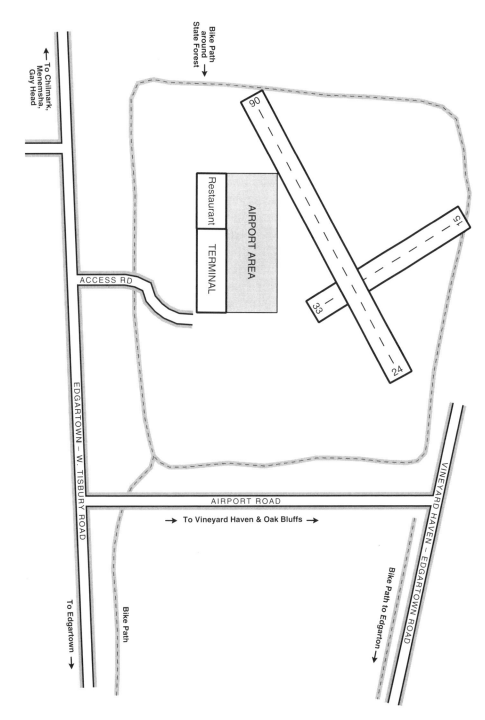

If You Go:

Hire a taxi from the Vineyard Haven airport to Long Point, the beach just opposite the airport entrance. If the driver is unfamiliar, tell him it is Trustees of Reservations land. This is really only a 2 1/2-mile cab ride, and there should be room for negotiation in the fare. Have him drop you off at the parking lot and arrange to have him pick you up a few hours later. Enjoy the surf side of Long Point Beach, but also swim in Tisbury Great Pond. This is a saltwater pond that communicates with the ocean during some weeks in the spring and fall. The best swimming in Tisbury Great Pond is about a half-mile walk down the beach toward the west from the parking lot. The water is about 10 to 15 degrees warmer in the pond and very calm. Alternate between the powerful surf and the relaxing salt pool for an enjoyable afternoon. Take a freshwater shower back at the parking lot, and you can desalinate, making your return plane ride more comfortable.

If you still have some energy back at the plane, break out the in-line skates to try out on the bike path around the perimeter of the airport. The path surface is smooth and the traffic is light. You may not want to go all the way around, though. It's more than 10 miles.

If you are looking for overnight accommodations on the Vineyard, you'll find a whole range of options. The most economical rooms are in and around Oak Bluffs, while the quaint inns of Edgartown are most expensive. Reservations are, of course, a good idea on a summer weekend.

Whatever your interests, you are sure to find that Martha's Vineyard is a special place, typically New England, but unique in its own right. Please see the other entries on Martha's Vineyard in this guide for more details.

Contacts:

Bicycle rental (in Edgartown)
    (508) 627-4052
    R.W. Cutler Bikes
    1 Main Street
    Edgartown, 02539

Airport Operations
    (508) 693-7022

Martha's Vineyard Chamber of Commerce
    (508) 693-0085
    Beach Road, P.O. Box 1698
    Vineyard Haven 02568

All Island Rent-a-Car
 (508) 693-6868
 (to rent a four-wheel-drive vehicle)

Tradewinds Airport/Martha's Vineyard (Private)

Location: Tradewinds is in the town of West Tisbury on Martha's Vineyard (adjacent to Farm Neck Golf Course).

Airfield: Tradewinds is a small, turf, VFR airfield. This is a private field, owned by the Land Bank of Martha's Vineyard. Permission to land here can be obtained in writing. (Details are listed below.) Aircraft overnight parking is not permitted. There are no lights at either of the two intersecting runways, and no airport services are available. The longer of the two runways, runway 6-24, is 2200 feet in length. The approach is fairly easy for a soft field, but has some undulations that may cause you to become airborne again after touchdown, making the aircraft difficult to control. The field conditions can be variable, but there is no one to call about this. I suggest a flyby to search for any obstacles or hazards. The shorter and intersecting runway, 13-31, is closed. There is no Unicom frequency for Tradewinds, but you should broadcast your intentions with Martha's Vineyard Tower as you approach the field. The controller can give you some information about the field and will separate you from the main airport traffic. This field uses a thousand-foot pattern with right-hand traffic on runway 24. There is no FBO here, and no facilities or rest rooms. The golf club is your best bet for assistance, if needed.

Activities: Primarily golf at the Farm Neck Golf Club

Background: If you want to play golf on Martha's Vineyard, this is your airport of entry. The clubhouse is just 100 yards from the designated aircraft parking area (see the map). Farm Neck Golf Club is without question the nicest course on Martha's Vineyard, and semi-private. It is open to the public with the exception of a few peak hours on summer weekend mornings. The greens fees are steep, about $75 per person on weekends. During the off-season, the rates are much more reasonable and the course is less crowded, as expected. The course is challenging without being frustratingly so

Farm Neck Golf Club, Martha's Vineyard.

and has some great water holes. The atmosphere is devoid of the snobbism that characterizes many other "exclusive" clubs. Calling ahead is almost mandatory for tee time reservation. The club has an excellent restaurant for lunch or dinner on weekends during the summer months. From the field, you are approximately 3 miles to the town of Oak Bluffs and 4 miles to Edgartown. There are no stores or restaurants within walking distance. This is ideal for a pure golf outing. otherwise, the two other airports of entry to Martha's Vineyard are available and more reliable.

Contacts:

For permission to land at Tradewinds, write to:
    Carolyn Cullen
    Airport Services Coordinator, P. O. Box 1953
    Vineyard Haven, MA 02568

Farm Neck Golf Club Pro Shop
    (508) 693-3057
    P.O. Box 1656
    Oak Bluffs, 02557

Farm Neck Restaurant/Café
    (508) 693-3560

Tradewinds Airport/Martha's Vineyard (B18)

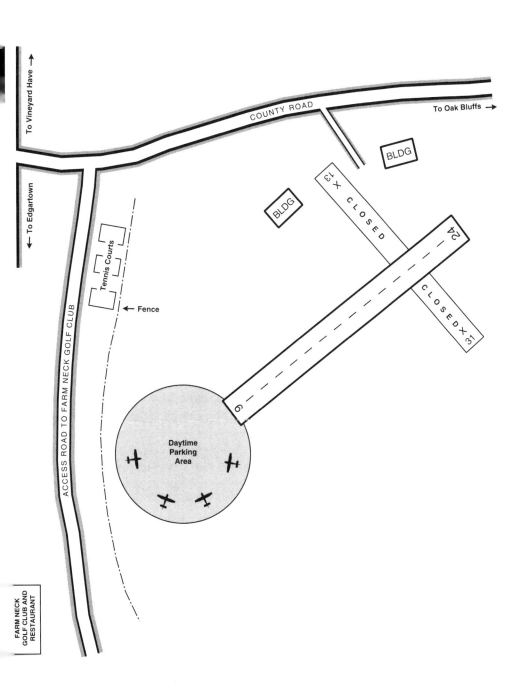

My sister and I on a Christmas stroll in Nantucket

Nantucket Airport (ACK)

Location: Twenty miles off the coast of southeast Cape Cod

Airfield: Nantucket Airport is easily approached, even for the inexperienced pilot. The option of three intersecting runways is sure to minimize the crosswind component, and the wide open airport area makes visibility and runway recognition straightforward. A variety of instrument approaches are available and the airport facilities are comprehensive. My only word of caution to the novice pilot landing at Nantucket concerns the weekend traffic load, especially Friday and Sunday. One Sunday morning I was "cleared to land, number <u>seven</u>!"

Activities:
1. Cycling
2. Shopping/dining
3. Beach activities
4. Boating

Background: Nantucket is clearly one of the most charming islands in this region. Because of its distance from the mainland, the ferry

Nantucket Airport (ACK)

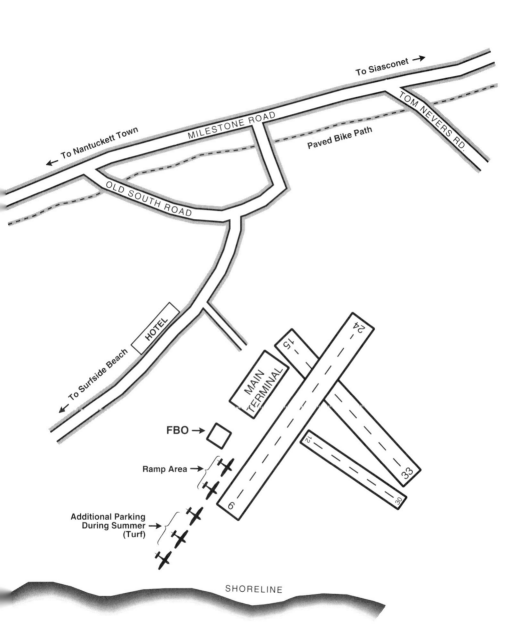

ride to Nantucket discourages day travelers, making it less crowded than some of the other islands. Most of the people heading to this island stay for a week, or at least a weekend. The island is more secluded than Martha's Vineyard and some people consider it more exclusive as well. There is only one main town on Nantucket, and it is tastefully New England. Restaurant prices are high, but most vacationers who frequent Nantucket are not concerned with a strict budget. There are many beautiful beaches here, but much of the land is still private with limited access.

Nantucket hosts several festivals during the year with themes centering on music, art, flowers, and sailing. The island community is well organized and cohesive. Like Martha's Vineyard, Nantucket has become so popular during the high summer season that many people prefer the off-season, and the result is that the off-season has become extended.

Numerous possibilities for overnight accommodations exist. The best way to approach this part of your trip is to ask a friend for a recommendation or to contact the chamber of commerce for a free guide. The chamber is very helpful, efficient, and accessible, and my sister works there. Ask for Tracy! (See Contacts below.)

For the cycling enthusiast, there are many miles of protected bicycle paths, some of which lead right to the beach. If you have always wanted to drive an over-sand vehicle, you can rent one right from the airport. Bicycle hire is not available from the airport. Instead, you must travel into town, a 10-minute, $8 cab ride. If you bring your own bicycles or in-line skates, a protected bike path starts less than a quarter of a mile from the airport access road. Believe it or not, there are some nice off-road mountain bike rides on this island. The central part, designated the Moors, is a complex network of inland dunes, dirt roads, and sand paths. The riding is strenuous but unique. There is the illusion that you are miles away from city stress when you ride here. These paths meander into cranberry bogs and island brush farther to the southeast. Despite the lack of change in elevation, the ride is rigorous and challenging. Road cycling is more popular on Nantucket.

If your main activity is at the ocean, then surf-side beach is only about a 10- or 15-minute walk from the airport. This is the shoreline that you pass over during the approach to runway 6. Physically, the shore is only about 200 yards from the threshold, but access to it is circuitous when traveling by foot or car.

Finally, if you are a shopper with an eye for fine collectibles

My two foldable bicycles. Starting out from Nantucket airport on a summer morning.

and antiques, Nantucket is your haven. Bring plenty of plastic, though, and head into town. If you are a "turbo" shopper then the airport will return your $7 landing/parking fee if your time on the ground is less than 2 hours.

If You Go:
Quit your job and choose a beautiful midweek summer day to fly to Nantucket! Take a taxi into town and rent a bicycle. Ask for directions to my favorite sandwich place in the whole world, Something Natural. Take your bicycle to this establishment, approximately 1 1/2 miles out of town on Cliff Road. Sit on the grass, rest and digest, and plan the rest of your day. Make your way to the bicycle path toward the north end of the island (See the map) and enjoy an afternoon at the beach, or come back into town and meander along the waterfront. You will see some beautiful yachts, and there are a number of restaurants with out-door seating where you can watch the boats come and go.

Want to skip the hustle and bustle of town? One of my favorite beaches is at the south end of the island, Siasconset. Conveniently, this beach is at the southern end of the bike path, which runs adja-cent to the airport. When you return to your plane at the general aviation pilot's lounge, you can shower and rinse away the salt prior to your return flight.

Contacts:

Nantucket Island Chamber of Commerce
(508) 228-1700
48 Main Street
Nantucket, 02564

Young's Bicycle Shop
(508) 228-1151
Steamboat Wharf
Nantucket, 02564

Something Natural sandwich shop
(508) 228-0504
50 Cliff Road
Nantucket, 02564

Jeep rental from the airport (Preston's)
(508) 228-0047 or (508) 228-4150

NEW HAMPSHIRE

Laconia (LCI)

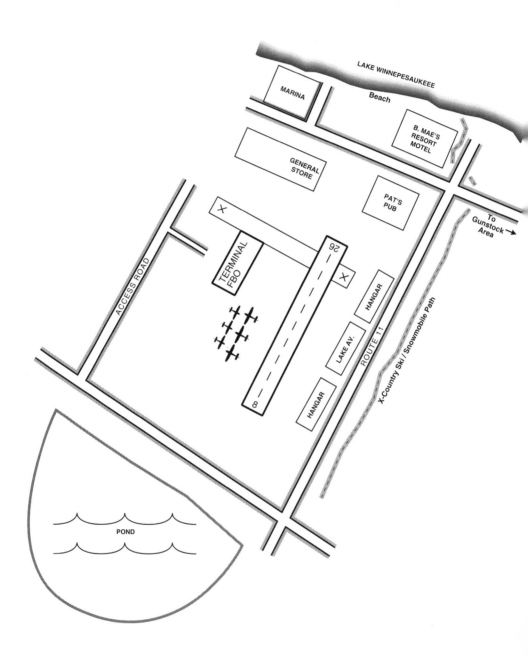

Laconia (LCI)

Location: The lakes region of central New Hampshire.

Airfield: The approach to Laconia is fairly easy. Although there is a few-hundred-foot peak just to the east of the runway 26 threshold, the airport area is vast with good visibility. The runway itself is long, wide, smooth, and well maintained year-round. The airport is very quiet most of the time, even in summer. Winter operations are not a problem either, as the local FBOs are functional through all seasons. Nonprecision instrument approaches are available. Parking is free, and employees of the local FBO are among the kindest and most helpful I have ever encountered.

Activities:
1. Mountain climbing
2. Hiking
3. Swimming
4. Boating
5. Downhill skiing
6. Cross-country skiing
7. Ice fishing

Background: Laconia is a great place to visit in all seasons. Activities are numerous for people of all ages who enjoy the outdoors. This area of the White Mountain National Forest is south of any major mountain range. What makes it special is Lake Winnipesaukee, an extensive and beautiful natural resource. One of America's first resort areas, this lake is famous for landlocked salmon fishing as well as other water sports. Many of the towns along the lake are built up, but the area has still retained its New England charm and beauty. Summer traffic around the lake can be heavy, but you can find peaceful surroundings, especially if you inquire at one of the many general stores along the way. The lake is remarkably clean in most spots, and due to its jagged shoreline and many coves, you can expect a reasonable amount of privacy while on the water.

About 5 miles from Laconia airport is Gunstock Mountain, a popular intermediate downhill ski area. This is a great family spot for downhill and cross-country skiing during the midwinter months. The elevation is low in comparison with some of the other moun-

A cross country adventure from Laconia airport.

tains in the area, so be sure to check conditions. There are cut trails for cross-country skiers here at this designated area.

While Laconia is not the most beautiful town in the Lakes Region, it does offer convenience and a great place to begin your summer or winter flying adventure. Boat rental is also possible from nearby marinas, within walking distance. If you desire to be less active, and just want some lunch, a favorite watering hole is Patrick's Pub just east of the end of runway 26. This establishment offers shuttle service in a big white limousine to pilots and their guests during certain times of the year.

If You Go:
Summer: Take the bicycle you brought or a courtesy car to Lookout Mountain or Gunstock Mountain recreational area. Both of these offer a relatively easy climb or day hike. The most rewarding aspect of this activity will be that when you get no more than halfway up you will be able to see a beautiful vista of Lake Winnipesaukee and the surrounding White Mountains, weather permitting. There are plenty of places to picnic along the way, if you climb Gunstock.

On your way back to the airport, stop at Patrick's Pub and sit out on the deck for a refreshment or some appetizers. If its a warm day, walk across the street from Patrick's to the marina and pretend to head for your private yacht. There is a nice beach, roped off for swimmers, just adjacent to the dock area. I have never been alerted to the fact that this is a private marina, for boat owners only, but I know this is the case. The water here is safe and relatively clean and refreshing. There is nothing like a dip in the lake before your flight back home.

Winter: Park your plane across the runway from the main terminal area. There should be ample parking available in the winter. If you have any questions, just look for the LAKE AIRCRAFT sign. On the opposite side of the main road, Route 11, which runs parallel to runway 08-26, is a snowmobile trail. This trail leads alongside the road down to the lake. Cross-country ski down to the lake on this trail. Cross the street and continue behind B-Mae's Resort Hotel. You will find another network of trails, leading directly onto the lake. Try skiing out on the lake (if you can tolerate the cold). You have to pick and choose your days to do this, because the wind can be impressive. Stop at one of the ice fishing huts to say hello or inquire about the daily catch. These people are friendly and usually eager to talk to anyone. You can also explore some of the smaller islands within skiing distance. Very often, there is an abundance of snowmobile tracks, which makes the skiing fast and easy. Come back for hot coffee or soup at Patrick's Pub, now open year-round.

For accommodations, B-Mae's place always has vacancies. This is convenient to the airport, but the next step up, in terms of comfort, is around the Gunstock area. A number of bed & breakfasts as well as small inns exist. The Wolfeboro Inn is my favorite, a 20-minute drive around the lake to the east. Wolfeboro has its own airport, but no transportation facilities, and it is still 3 miles away from town. (See the separate entry on Wolfeboro.)

Contacts:

Sky Bright Aviation (local FBO)
    (603) 528-6818 or (800) 639-6012
    P.O. Box 7405
    Gilford, 03247

Patrick's Pub
    (603) 293-0841
    18 Wiers Road
    Gilford, 03246

B-Mae's Resort
    (603) 293-7526 or (800) 458-3877
    17 Harris Shore Road, Route 11
    Gilford, 03246

Moultonboro (NH08)

Location: On the northern tip of Lake Winnipesaukee, Lakes Region

Airfield: The field is a smooth-surface, asphalt, 3000-foot runway. The approach is relatively easy in conditions of good visibility. There is a nonprecision instrument approach available. The field is privately owned, and there is a landing fee of $7, but nothing more than fuel, a pay phone, and an outhouse for facilities. The folks that run the operations at Moultonboro Airport go out of their way to help you. Several times they have offered to drive me to my destination and one Sunday night I found myself at Moultonboro with mechanical problems. To make a long story short, I took a ride back to Boston from one of these fine gentlemen. It was a case of one aviator helping another and just another reason why I like this place so much.

Activities:
1. Bird watching
2. Walking
3. Cross-country skiing
4. Mountain biking

Background: Moultonboro is one of several small private airports in this region, and probably the least well known. There is no real metropolis here, but the area is quite beautiful. For the birder, there is the Loon Center, a small recreational area where you can walk through the woods along a lakeshore in search of waterfowl in the relaxing state of mind we experience too infrequently. This preserve is a 10-minute walk from the Old Orchard Inn, a lovely country bed & breakfast that features an antique shop within the same establishment. Across the street from the inn is an excellent restaurant for dinner, the Woodshed, making this area convenient for the traveler without an automobile. The innkeepers will pick you up at the airport, approximately 2 1/2 miles from the inn. One mile from the airport is the Moultonboro General Store, an institution in and of

Moultonboro (NH08)

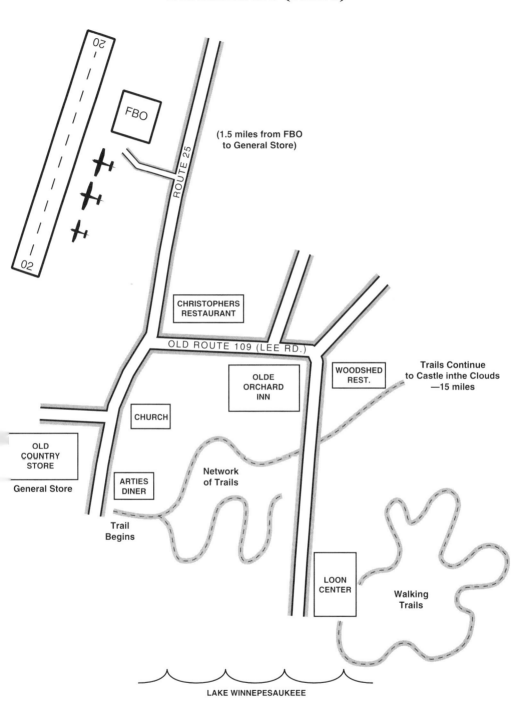

20

FBO

ROUTE 25

(1.5 miles from FBO
to General Store)

02

CHRISTOPHERS
RESTAURANT

OLD ROUTE 109 (LEE RD.)

OLDE
ORCHARD
INN

WOODSHED
REST.

Trails Continue
to Castle inthe Clouds
—15 miles

CHURCH

OLD
COUNTRY
STORE

General Store

ARTIES
DINER

Network
of Trails

Trail
Begins

LOON
CENTER

Walking
Trails

LAKE WINNEPESAUKEEE

itself. This store sells everything from antique furniture to Native American souvenirs to White Mountain trail guides and maple syrup. This place is definitely worth a half hour of your time, even if you don't "need anything." Across the street from the general store is a diner-style sandwich shop, Artie's. Behind Artie's is a network of trails through a heavily wooded area that eventually leads to Castle in the Clouds, a well-known tourist spot. The castle is something to see once, but the trails can provide you with many afternoons of exercise and enjoyment. I have cycled this area with a mountain bike and been cross-country skiing here as well. It is a perfect place for either.

If You Go:

Make reservations for an overnight stay at the Old Orchard Inn. There are bicycles here for guests, but don't expect state-of-the-art machines. Walk or ride to the Loon Center and visit the store on the premises. If you choose a winter visit to Moultonboro, bring your cross-country skis. Enter the path behind Artie's sandwich shop and take an out-and-back trek through the woods. Come back for 3 o'clock tea at the inn and then eat dinner across the street at the Woodshed. Don't forget to stop at the General Store for some local memorabilia or gifts for the family.

Contacts:

Olde Orchard Inn
    (603) 476-5004 or (800) 598-5845
    R.R. Box 256
    Moultonboro, 03254

Moultonboro Airport
    (603) 476-8801
    Route 25
    Moultonboro, 03254

Woodshed Restaurant
    (603) 476-2311
    Lee's Mill Road
    Moultonboro, 03254

Wolfeboro (Lakes Region) (8B8)

Location: Wolfeboro sits on the southeast shore of Lake Winnipesaukee, in the Lakes Region

Airfield: Wolfeboro has a 2000-foot, newly paved (1997) runway, that slopes down toward the northwest. Fuel is available, and the runway is lit for night use, but there are no instrument approaches here. The visual approach is straightforward, and when approaching from the east, runway 30, the only problem is clearance of some trees. From the other direction, runway 12, the runway's threshold is just beyond the water's edge, so a low approach is much more feasible. The approach is easy to spot from all directions by looking for the projection of Wolfeboro, which juts out into the lake. Once you identify this, you will see the runway carved out of this island-type land mass. Laconia Airport is just a few miles away, across Lake Winnipesaukee, and the FBO there can usually be raised on the radio for wind conditions. This is important, because Wolfeboro is often unattended. There are virtually no facilities at the Lakes Region airport, with the exception of fuel when attended, and a pay phone.

Activities:
1. Swimming
2. Lake cruises
3. Sailing
4. Fishing

Background: The town of Wolfeboro was incorporated in 1787 and is known as one of the first resort towns in America. That is to say, this area of Lake Winnipesaukee has been a favorite spot of New England families for centuries. In the early 20th century, it was popular for wealthy Bostonian families to travel here for summer recreation, by the largest lake in this region. Several of the adjacent towns have placed more emphasis on economic development and tourism, with less attention paid to the preservation of historical and natural beauty. Wolfeboro is not only one of the most well-known towns on Winnipesaukee, but it is also perhaps the prettiest.

The town sits 3 1/2-miles from the landing strip, and a winding road leads you from the airfield to the main street. (See map for details.)

Wolfeboro (Lakes Region) (8B8)

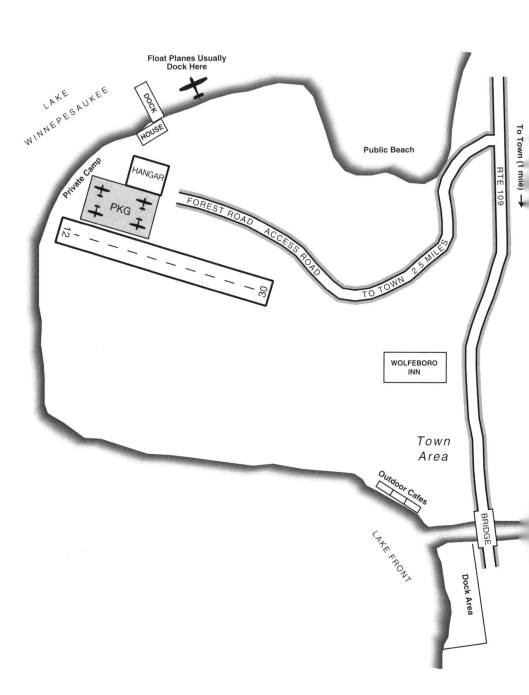

The town of Wolfeboro consists of one main street, lined with a few restaurants, and crafts and pottery shops. There is a small waterfront area adjacent to the dairy bar, which is a perfect place to sit and enjoy an ice cream or snack while watching the boats go by and the fishermen angle for landlocked salmon. The pace is slow, and the atmosphere is without pretense. Although this town boasts of being exclusive in terms of history and heritage, this is still central New Hampshire!

The Wolfeboro Inn is a great place to stay. If prearranged, someone will pick you up at the airport and bring you into town. The rooms are clean, relatively quiet, and reasonably priced. 2 restaurants are available at the inn. The first, Wolfe's, features a dimly lit, pub-style atmosphere. The other, the main dining room, is quite nice and, once again, very reasonably priced. The inn is on the edge of town, set back from the main commercial activity, but close enough to walk anywhere in town.

The greatest resource in this area is Lake Winnipesaukee. This body of water has many coves and much shoreline, which is beautiful to survey either from a boat or by air. Guided boat tours leave from town daily and are free with your stay at the Wolfeboro Inn. Around Wolfeboro, there are some elaborate waterfront properties with boathouses, which remind me of those I have seen on Lake Zurich. It's fun to take a leisurely cruise by these estates. You will undoubtedly come across some antique boats similar to those seen in the movie *On Golden Pond*.

If you have no interests in the town of Wolfeboro, but are looking for a quick dip in a clean and beautiful part of this large lake, this is your spot. The airport property includes a small house with a dock about 75 yards from the strip, just behind the main hangar. When I have asked the FBO attendants, they permit my friends and me to swim from the dock and sun ourselves there. The house is under construction, and there is usually a seaplane next to the dock. If there is no one at the airport, this is a good marker to indicate that you are at the right place on the waterfront.

If You Go:
Stop into Wolfeboro on a clear summer day, a lazy afternoon when you want to swim with friends. Take a dip from the dock behind the airport. Bring some towels and a picnic lunch and swim along the shore to your left. Just around the point is a beach, that is owned by a summer camp. This is a fine place to pause, rest, and sun yourself for a few moments before you return to your home-base dock.

Plan an overnight at the Wolfeboro Inn. Ask for transportation to and from the inn, and someone will come get you, as previously mentioned. Take a boat tour of the lake-explore some of the hidden coves and small islands. Have dinner in the main dining room at the Wolfeboro Inn, and then sit by the fireplace with a glass of wine in the Inn's lobby. Browse the fine pottery store across the street from the inn, approximately 50 yards toward town, where the artist/owner will proudly display her works. Otherwise, sitting lakeside at one of the 2 waterfront cafes in town is a great way to kill a couple of hours and is an effective stress management strategy as well!

Contacts:
The Wolfeboro Inn
    (603) 569-3016
    44 North Main Street
    Wolfeboro, 03894

The Wolfeboro Chamber of Commerce
    (800) 451-2389
    Railroad Avenue
    Wolfeboro, 03894

Lakes Region Airport
    (603) 569-1310
    Wolfeboro Neck
    Wolfeboro, 03894

Taxi
    (603) 569-1397

Mount Washington/Whitefield (HIE)

Location: White Mountains of New Hampshire

Airfield: Mount Washington Regional Airport is your best bet for an instrument approach into this part of the White Mountains. The 3500-foot strip is located in a valley north of several 6000-foot peaks. The flight over Mount Washington is spectacular on a clear day and alone is worth the trip. This is a very quiet place; of the many times I have landed here, only twice have I encountered fellow pilots at the GA pilot shack/headquarters. Occasionally, you can find people working on their planes or in nearby hangars, but there are virtually

The nature preserve behind the airport at Whitefield, with Mt. Washington in the background.

no FBO services available aside from a phone and a toilet. One time, I flew here in winter, 3 days after a snowstorm. The runway had not been plowed, and there were no NOTAMS indicating this was the case. I made a flyby and landed at another airport in the region. The point is, services are limited here and although this is one of the longer and wider runways in the area, use caution and do not rely on anyone on the ground for assistance. It is possible to hire a taxi from the field, but it comes from the adjacent town of Littleton.

Activities:
1. Fishing
2. Walking
3. Hiking
4. Mountain biking
5. Cross-country skiing

Background: Mount Washington/Whitefield is a spot worth exploring, although some degree of self-sufficiency is required. The surroundings are picturesque, with a backdrop of the White Mountains,

Mount Washington/Whitefield (HIE)

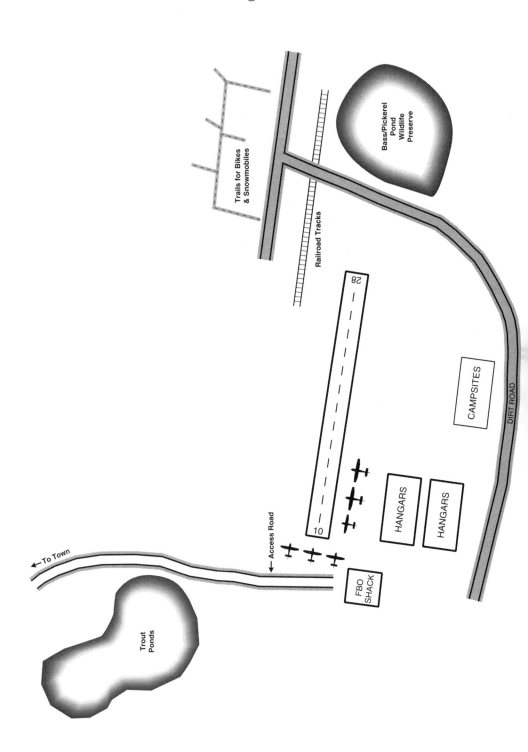

Flying over the White Mountains on a winter afternoon.

and much of the area around the field is conservation land. On the
south side of the runway, behind the hangars, you will find a dirt
road. Following this road east leads to a network of trails and power
lines. On the right side of the railroad tracks, there is a beautiful
pond with good bass and pickerel fishing. During the winter months,
you will see snowmobiles (and the occasional cross-country skier)
coursing up and down the power-line trails. In summer, this same
locale is ideal for a leisurely afternoon walk. There is even a camping
area at the beginning of this dirt road, off to the left as you face east.

In the opposite direction, heading west, a pond runs along the
access road to the airport. This is a prime spot for trout. I have seen
several fish taken here, brown trout, and I am told that this pond is
stocked frequently during the season. Beware, though. I would imagine that there is regular surveillance by the authorities in making
sure you have a New Hampshire fishing license. This can be
obtained at the village gun store in the town of Whitefield.

Whitefield is about a 3-mile trip from the airport. It is an easy
bike ride and quite typical of a sleepy little town in central New
Hampshire. There are a couple of good restaurants nearby for lunch
and brunch. Barbara's and Country Vittles both offer wholesome
"rib-sticking" food.

If You Go:
Plan a camping overnight to Mount Washington Regional. Set up your campsite just adjacent to the field on the south side behind the hangars in the designated area. Bring your own bicycles and take a ride into town west on Route 3 toward Whitefield. Have lunch or brunch at Barbara's Little Restaurant. Stop in town to pick up a fishing license at the gun store. When you return to the airfield, have a walk along the trails in back of the field or try some evening trout fishing. No luck there? The pond on the south side of the dirt road just after you pass the railroad tracks has some very large pickerel. These are easier to catch, although not as tasty. Enjoy the trout that you have caught for dinner, but if you are like me, you will probably have a backup plan just in case the big one gets away!

Contacts:
The Inn at Whitefield (open year round)
    (603) 837-2760
    Route 3
    Whitefield, 03598

Barbara's Little Restaurant
    (603) 837-3161
    Route 3
    Whitefield, 03598

Local information for field conditions (seasonal)
    (603) 837-2627

Franconia (1B5)

Location: Franconia is a small town nestled in the White Mountains approximately 20 miles west of Mount Washington.

Airfield: The field is a 2600-foot turf strip oriented north-south, lying just north of a ridge of 6000-foot peaks. For this reason, a quick descent is necessary if you are approaching from the south and do not wish to circle the area prior to landing. The runway threshold is frequently displaced, which may cause the length of the runway to vary a few hundred feet. The field is well maintained and sufficiently wide, though, and aside from the usual precautions concerning mountain flying, it is not particularly difficult to land at. As

Gliders at Franconia.

you consult your VFR chart, look for the field and adjacent tennis courts as well as 2 large buildings across the street from this area. Beware of glider activities: The FBO offers this service nonstop during beautiful summer days, especially on weekends. You will see private soaring enthusiasts as well as rides for hire. The folks who run the FBO are helpful and usually available during daylight hours. Remember, this is a VFR airport with no lights, day use only.

Activities:
1. Gliding/soaring
2. Horseback riding
3. Mountain biking
4. Robert Frost Museum
5. Hiking the Appalachian Trail

Background: Franconia is my favorite spot in New Hampshire. I can't think of a more beautiful place on earth during peak foliage season, as I'll describe over the next few pages. This is really a special place, but, as you can imagine, a trip here requires that you have the cooperation of Mother Nature.

Across from the field is the Franconia Inn, a moderately priced country inn with a lovely restaurant, pool, and clay tennis courts. There is nothing pretentious about this place, and the pace is slow and relaxing. Adjacent to the inn is a riding center, which facilitates guided horseback tours in the summer and cross-country skiing in winter. Arrangements can be made for both of these activities at the Franconia Inn, even if you are not staying there. The inn also has bicycles, free of charge, for nearby trail riding or a quick jaunt into town. The town is approximately 3 miles along the main road, Route 116, to the north. There is not much to see in Franconia, nor is this a shopping mecca, but a few restaurants, a general store, and a great bakery may make it worth the short bike ride.

1 mile south of the airport, along the left side of Route 116, you will find a favorite place for hiking and walking. The Copper Mine Trail, part of the Appalachian Trail, winds along side a beautiful brook. The gradual climb of 2 1/2 miles is perfect for a family afternoon outing, not too strenuous or technical, but some great exercise nevertheless. Your reward for making it to the top is a splendid waterfall and natural pool beneath. There is even a small area for camping just beneath the falls with a roofed shelter. I really love this place. I have been there every year since I discovered it and in all seasons, with the exception of midwinter.

Just prior to the Copper Mine Trail head (at the bottom) is a network of trails through the woods. These are equestrian paths used by the riding center, but mountain bikers have taken to them as well. Hybrid off-road bikes are available from the Franconia Inn at no charge to guests. These trails are a bit too technical for the bikes available. I suggest renting some heavy-duty cycles from in town for off-road riding in this area.

As you head into town from the inn, less than 1 mile on the left-hand side along Route 116, you will see signs for the Robert Frost Museum. This is the house where Frost spent summers in his younger years. The inside is unimpressive, but the grounds behind the property involve a nature walk with poem plaques nicely displayed on trees along the way. This is fascinating for the Frost enthusiast and poetry buff. The experience combines nature with poetry in a unique way.

If You Go:
Fly to Franconia for a summer overnight. Make reservations at the Franconia Inn, and ask for a room with a view. Take a walk up the

Franconia (1B5)

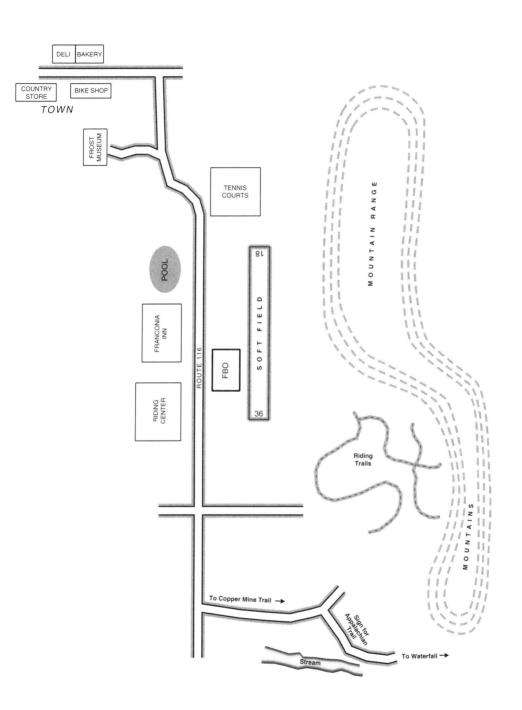

The Franconia Inn

Copper Mine Trail and enjoy a picnic lunch at the falls. Return to the
inn for a game of tennis or to just relax by the pool. Dine at the inn
and ask the staff there to help you plan your next day. Go horseback
riding, soaring, or even take a simple bike ride into town for some
fresh baked goods at the Greatful Bread Bakery. On your way back
from town, stop at the Robert Frost Museum for an hour of educational and cultural enrichment.

Contacts:
Franconia Inn
  (603) 823-5542 Or (800) 473-5299
  Route 116, Easton Road
  Franconia, 03580

Franconia Airfield FBO and Soaring Center
  (603) 823-8881

The Frost Place (Robert Frost Museum)
  (603) 823-5510
  P.O. Box F
  Franconia, 03580

Twin Mountain (8B2)

Location: Twin Mountain is nestled among the White Mountains in central New Hampshire.

Airfield: This paved, 2600-foot air strip, which is 1459 feet above sea level, can be predictably challenging to land at. It is relatively narrow and surrounded by trees. Nevertheless, in good visibility and light winds, there is nothing to fear here. Beware of the downslope to runway 27 and the implications that this configuration has on creating the illusion of being higher than you actually are. Although the airport has pilot-controlled lighting, apparently airport officials have the authority to restrict the use of the field at night, if they deem it unsafe.

Activities:
1. Hiking
2. Climbing
3. Photography

Background: Twin Mountain Airfield is the perfect spot to begin a day hike in the White Mountains. The Appalachian Trail runs just adjacent to the airport, and you can begin trips of varying length and degree of difficulty. The views are spectacular at different points, and the trail is suitable for children and experienced hikers alike.

Close to the airport area are camping facilities as well as small and inexpensive motels. This trip is mainly a camping and hiking experience, so don't expect to discover a nearby town with shopping outlets, there won't be any. The airport is strictly VFR and should be reserved for those predictable days when high pressure dominates.

If You Go:
Get yourself an Appalachian Mountain Club (AMC) map and guide. These can be obtained at any of the New England camping establishments, Eastern Mountain Sports (EMS), REI, L.L. Bean, for example, or by writing to the address below. This map will show you the Sugarloaf Trail, which starts just behind the airport property. The trail has proximity to a stream and offers a short climb, 1000 feet vertical, to a ridge where magnificent views dominate. At one end of the Sugarloaf Trail is a campground for overnight stays. 1 mile beyond

Twin Mountain (8B2)

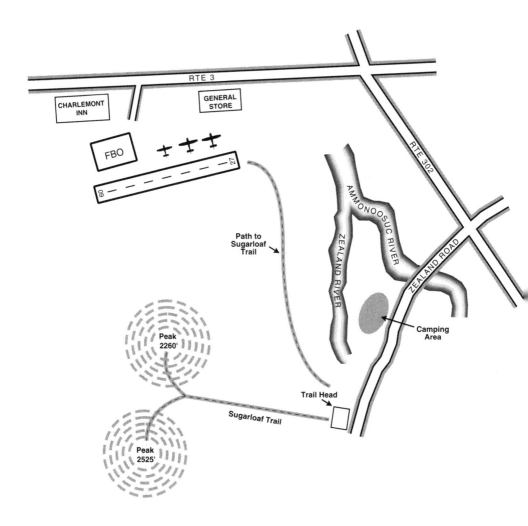

this campground brings you to the base of Mount Hale, if you desire a more invigorating 8-mile loop climb. This could be the second day of a two-day expedition or the second part of a very long day of hiking!

If you want to do the hike but are not in the mood for camping or have strong feelings about a hot shower at the end of each day, try the Charlemont Hotel adjacent to the airfield. The accommodations are spartan, but the price is right. Don't expect elegant dining, either, but this may be a perfect opportunity to bring your own gourmet sandwiches in a cooler. Sometimes it is more fun that way!

Beware of the rumor that a courtesy car is available. I did not find this to be the case either time I visited Twin Mountain. Call ahead if you have any questions.

Contacts:
Charlemont Motor Inn
    (603) 846-5549
    US Route 3, P.O. Box G
    Twin Mountain, 03595
Twin Mountain Airport
    (603) 846-5505
    P.O. Box 97
    Twin Mountain, 03595
Appalachian Trail Conference
    (304) 535-6331
    P.O. Box 807
    Harpers Ferry, WV 25425

Jaffrey—Silver Ranch (AFN)

Location: South-central New Hampshire

Airfield: Jaffrey is a quiet airport with multiple nonprecision approaches. The visual approach to this 3000-foot paved runway is straightforward. There are no major obstacles here, but the low, surrounding hills provide for some gusty winds on final approach. The folks at the local FBO are extremely kind, courteous, and eager to help you. Transportation to and from the field is limited, and taxi is your best bet, unless you have made other arrangements. (See suggestions below.)

Activities:
1. Hiking
2. Mountain climbing
3. Horseback riding

Background: Jaffrey is a small town, not well known to weekend vacationers, but it is the gateway to the Monadnock region for the general aviation pilot. The field is open year-round, and winter activities including cross-country skiing and sleigh riding make it interesting to come here in the off-season. By far the most popular time to visit this area is during the peak foliage season. Spectacular colors are seen at this time, and weekend leaf-peepers flock to this region for the great show. This is also the land of covered bridges, as the Connecticut River winds its way through this part of New Hampshire.

Across Route 124 from the airport entrance is the Silver Ranch. Here you can find a variety of equestrian activities, summer and winter. The warm weather affords carriage rides, hayrides, and trail rides. In the wintertime, sleigh rides and cross-country skiing make for a brisk and enjoyable afternoon.

Less than 10 miles from the Silver Ranch Air Park is the entrance to Monadnock State Park. Here you'll discover one of the most climbed mountains in North America, perfect for an afternoon hike, approximately 4 hours of exercise round-trip. The trails are clearly marked and well kept up. They are marked according to difficulty and offer a range of challenge and skill level. Whichever trail you choose, you are sure to be rewarded with spectacular views.

The Benjamin Prescott Inn is a bed & breakfast located approximately three-quarters of a mile from the airport, south on Route 124. Hosts Barry and Janice will plan your entire weekend if you let them. They will pick you up at the airport and transport you to dinner at a restaurant of your choice. These folks are kind and genuine.

Nine-tenths of a mile from the airfield is Michael's Jaffrey Manor, a restaurant with local flavor and prices that can't be beat. This is a popular Sunday brunch spot. If you call ahead, transportation is provided to and from the airport. On the other hand, a leisurely walk (at least one way) may be preferable to alleviate some of the guilt caused by overeating! Brunch is still less than $10 here, and the owner/chef (Michael) is guaranteed to impress with the spread he puts on.

Jaffrey—Silver Ranch (AFN)

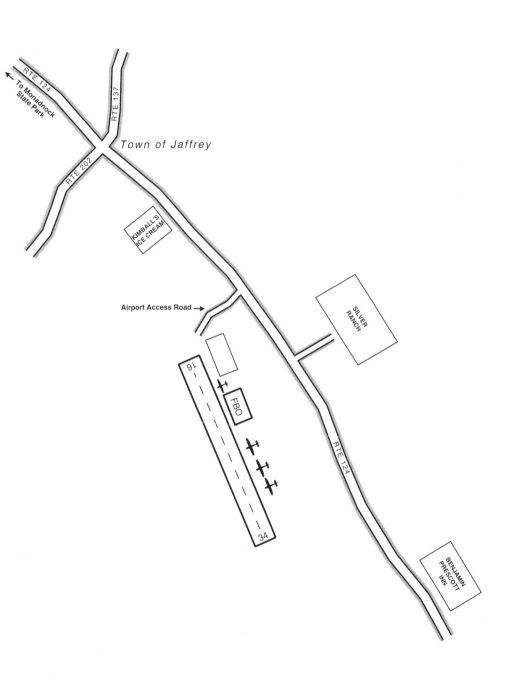

Finally, if you are looking for a quick stop to stretch your legs and grab an ice cream cone, Kimball's dairy bar is not more than one-tenth of a mile from the end of the runway. There is a picnic area out front-a great place to share or plan aviation adventures.

If You Go:
Visit Jaffrey-Silver Ranch in the autumn. Phone ahead to make arrangements with your hosts at the Benjamin Prescott Inn. Have these folks pick you up and even make your dinner reservations for you. Depending on the season, go for a sleigh ride, a hayride, or a trail ride at the Silver Ranch. If it is a beautiful day, the ranch is within walking distance of the inn. The next day, you can head for a day hike up Mount Monadnock. Walking shoes are necessary; serious hiking gear is optional.

Contacts:
Jaffrey-Silver Ranch Airpark
    (603) 532-8870 or (603) 532-7763
    Route 124
    Jaffrey, 03452

The Benjamin Prescott Inn
    (603) 532-6637
    Route 124 East
    Jaffrey, 03452

Monadnock State Park
    (603) 532-8862

The Boiler House at Noon Falls Restaurant
    (603) 924-9486
    Route 202 South
    Peterboro, 03458

Silver Ranch
    (603) 532-7363
    Route 124
    Jaffrey, 03452

Michael's Jaffrey Manor
    (603) 532-8555
    East Main Street
    Jaffrey, 03452

RHODE ISLAND

Newport State (UUU)

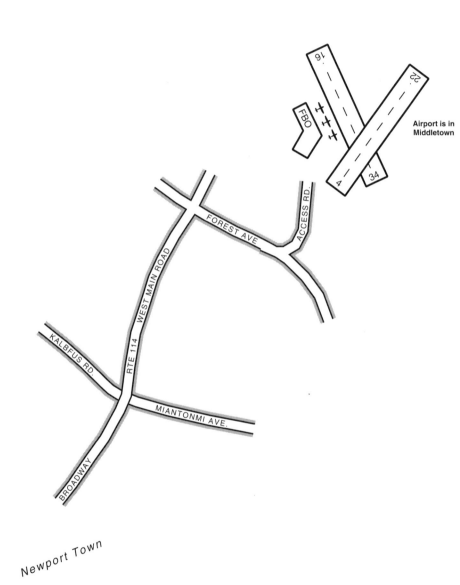

Newport State (UUU)

Location: Coastal Rhode Island

Airfield: Newport State offers 2 intersecting runways, the longer of which is 3000 feet. A variety of nonprecision instrument approaches are available (LOC, VOR, GPS). The visual approach is open and straightforward. Transportation is available at the airport, including taxis and rental cars. There is an FBO here with an active flight school, and it is not uncommon to encounter multiple aircraft practing in the pattern. Nevertheless, this field is relatively quiet and user-friendly, even in high summer.

Activities:
1. Beach activities
2. Newport mansions
3. Music festivals
4. Sailing
5. Horseback riding (beach)

Background: Newport is considered America's yachting capital. In addition to hosting the America's Cup and the tall ships, this historic seaport is where the U.S. Navy began. The Vanderbilts, the Astors, and the Morgans were successful in establishing Newport as a seaside summer resort for the most wealthy American families. The 10-mile ocean drive that winds along the Aquidneck Peninsula is your best terrestrial view of the beautiful homes lining Newport's coast, new and old. On a beautiful day, however, it is more enjoyable to view this coastal splendor using two other modes of transportation. The first is a flyby along the coast at 1000 feet. Please use extreme caution because you can bet other pilots have the same idea and may not be broadcasting their intentions. Every GA pilot flying in this region should see the mansions by air: It is one of the benefits.

Another way to experience Newport is by foot. The Cliff Walk is also a nice way to visit a few of these estates. A paved path runs behind the Bellevue Avenue mansions for about 3 1/2 miles. At least 2 miles of it is concrete, level, and easy walking. The last part involves climbing over some rocks and through tunnels, but is by no means an alpine expedition!

There is no paucity of great restaurants in Newport and no shortage of ambience at these places. A few I can recommend are The

Black Pearl, which overlooks the harbor and has a great outdoor patio in the summertime. The Mooring is perhaps the best harborside spot. This used to be the New York Yacht Club and it has an outdoor patio, but on a cooler day, it is nice to sit inside by the big windows and the huge fireplace. This is a great place for brunch, but my favorite brunch spot sits on a hill overlooking Narragansett Bay with a splendid view. The Inn at Castle Hill is famous for Sunday jazz brunch and is quite a social scene. Plan to wait for Sunday seating. On the even more elegant side, the Clarke Cooke House features fine food with ambience and attitude to match.

Newport has a very active chamber of commerce that organizes several festivals during the year. There are both folk and jazz festivals in the summer (and these weekends are perhaps the busiest) but many inns, restaurants, and shops are open year-round. There is even a winter festival in mid-February.

It is a good idea to reserve accommodations in Newport, especially during the high season. The Cliffside Inn is an excellent choice for a romantic getaway. The Hotel Viking is centrally located and convenient to a variety of in-town activities. There is great shopping along Thames Street, with its brick marketplace. Most places you can stay at provide a guide for specifics of in-town activities.

Beach activities are popular at Newport. First and Second Beach are perhaps the most well known, but they can be crowded during the summer. Goose Bay Beach is more secluded, but a bit harder to get to. Rose Island Lighthouse is a nice place to visit as well.

If You Go:
Visit Newport in the summer or late fall, depending on your level of tolerance for crowds. The summer crowd is young, with a heavy population of college students, and can get rowdy. You can avoid crowds by staying at some of the more remote bed & breakfasts. As previously mentioned, a flyby of the mansions is mandatory, at least once. Some of the experiences I would not forgo include Sunday jazz brunch at one of the places suggested, as well as the Cliff Walk and a visit to at least one mansion. These are really impressive and a variety of literature is available about them. This is an easy place to arrange for an afternoon sail, or even a harbor cruise. If you are a yachting aficionado, a tour of the harbor or bay will flame this passion.

Contacts:

The Newport County Convention & Visitors Bureau
(401) 849-8098 or (800) 326-6030
23 America's Cup Avenue

The Hotel Viking
(401) 847-3300 or (800) 556-7126

Taxi from Newport State Airport (Cozy Cab)
(401) 846-1500

(Hertz) rental car from Newport State Airport
(401) 846-1645

Cliffside Inn
(401) 847-1811 or (800) 845-1811
2 Seaview Avenue

Inn at Castle Hill
(401) 849-3800
Ocean Avenue

Adirondack schooner (afternoon sailing expedition)
(401) 846-1600

America's Cup Adventures (charter yachts)
(401) 848-5123

Block Island (BID)

Location: Ten miles off the coast

Airfield: While the strip at Block Island is relatively short (2500 feet) the approach is not difficult. The landing surface is very wide, open, and smooth. The only real concern in landing here is low-level wind shear on a gusty day. Nonprecision approaches are available.

Activities:
1. Touring by moped
2. Cycling
3. Beach activities

Background: Block Island is ideal for both a summer day trip and a weekend. Located off the coast of Rhode Island, this popular sum-

Lighthouse on Block Island.

mer vacation spot attracts more people from New York and Connecticut than from Massachusetts or other points northeast. As with
most uncontrolled airports, summer traffic can be unnerving and
requires a cool head and keen eye for traffic separation. Once you
land at the field, the town is only a mile away. The walk is not
scenic; you may want to hire a taxi for the short trip.

There are a number of pub-style restaurants in town for brunch,
lunch, or dinner, but in general Block Island falls behind Martha's
Vineyard and Nantucket for elegant and sophisticated dining. During
the summer months, on weekends, the ferry area is usually buzzing
with activity, and you may want to avoid this altogether. Bicycle
and moped rentals are available right in town. This is one of the few
places where I actually would recommend moped rental. Although
the island is only 10 miles long, there are steep hills and numerous
changes in elevation that may frustrate the cyclist who is looking for
low-level exercise. The main roads on Block Island are suitable for
moped travel and motorists are generally courteous. In the summer,
traffic is tolerable. All of these points factor into my recommendation for moped travel as relatively safe. On the other hand, a bicycle
is also a nice way to enjoy the flavor of this island. You do not have
to tour the entire island to experience this haven. (See If You Go.) As

Block Island (BID)

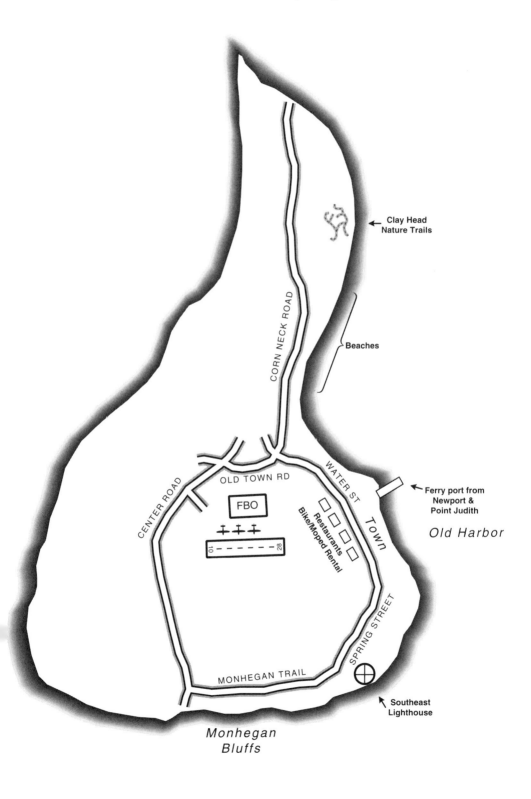

you tour the island, be prepared to stop frequently to relish the views.

Recently, the inns and hotels on the island have launched a campaign to boost tourism in the off-season. For those who do not mind the blustery weather, this is an ideal spot for a late-fall getaway. It will be quiet, peaceful, and economically favorable to stay at even one of the most elegant inns. A variety of package deals are available. The Hotel Manisses is an example of one such place, but several others are just as good.

There is quite a bit of history to this island, as it was first settled in the 1600s. The architecture is interesting, and the landscapes are unspoiled due to thoughtful and careful development, for the most part. The beaches are beautiful, and several nature preserves are perfect for an afternoon walk. The best way to find these is to ask at the bike or moped shop or to ask your innkeeper.

If You Go:

Choose a late September or early October day. Hire some bicycles or mopeds from town and head south toward the southeast lighthouse. Leave your bikes at the side of the road and walk along the cliffs at the lighthouse area. Head back toward town and stop for lunch at one of the pub-style restaurants. I suggest the Mohegan Café. After lunch, head north along the main road out of town. By utilizing the map obtained at the bicycle or moped rental shop, you can choose one of a several access roads to the beaches on the east side of the island. Proceeding north, you will also find some beautiful beach areas.

For accommodations, try the Hotel Manisses or the Atlantic Inn. Both are out of town and offer off-season rates. Both have lovely views but, the grounds at the Manisses are more extensive.

Contacts:

Hotel Manisses
    (401) 466-2421 or (800) MANISSES
    Spring Street
    Old Harbor
    Block Island, 02807

The Atlantic Inn
    (401) 466-5883 or (800) 224-7422
    High Street
    Old Harbor
    Block Island, 02807

Bicycle/moped rental (The Moped Man)
(401) 466-5444
435 Water Street
Old Harbor
Block Island, 02807

Block Island Chamber of Commerce
(401) 466-2982 or (800) 383-BIRI
Water Street
Old Harbor
Block Island, 02807

VERMONT

Mount Snow/West Dover (4V8)

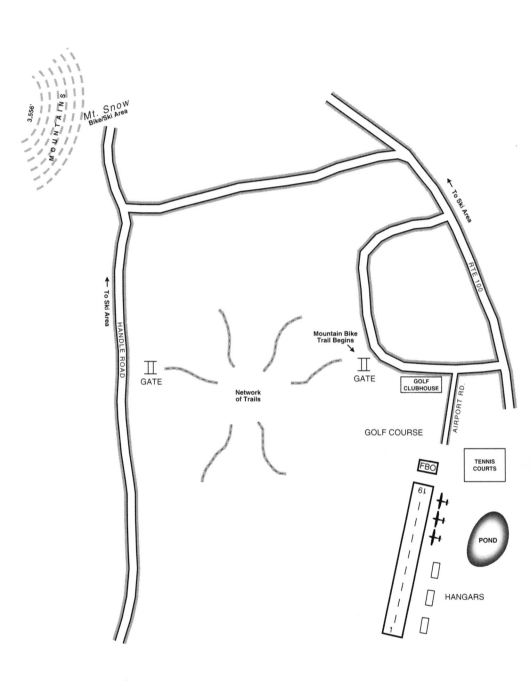

Mount Snow/West Dover (4V8)

Location: West Dover is in southern Vermont, just south of the Green Mountains

Airfield: This 2600-foot paved strip nestled in mountainous terrain should be regarded with appropriate caution. The approach to runway 01 from the south is a lot easier than its reciprocal approach, as the threshold area is open and there are no major ranges to cross from this direction. Wind shear from the variation in terrain makes it predictably difficult, so morning and evening landings are recommended. Airport services are available in all seasons, as is a courtesy car, although unreliably so. The best advice is to speak personally with the airport manager for availability and updated status of this service. The airport is well-maintained, staffed and plowed in the winter, and attended as advertised in the summer. Taxi service is also available from the airport, but pre-arrangements are necessary. Mount Snow is really an air park with a few facilities worthy of note. There are tennis courts here, available to guests who pay the landing fee, and a small pond with benches and chairs. This field is a nice place to stop for an hour to stretch, nap, or picnic.

Activities:
1. Golf
2. Tennis
3. Skiing
4. Mountain biking
5. Gourmet dining

Background: Mount Snow Airport is one of the few ski area-based fields in the Northeast. The mountain has sufficient elevation and variety of trails to make it challenging, and it is also an excellent place for a family outing. West Dover is less well developed than areas such as Killington and Sunday River. Nevertheless, you'll find a wide variety of accommodations. The base lodge is just a few miles from the airstrip and ground transportation can be arranged.

The warmer seasons in West Dover offer a variety of activities. There is a golf course within walking distance of the airfield. This is an excellent course, and accessible to nonmember's.

Another popular activity for the summer visitor to Mount Snow is mountain biking. There are 2 areas for trail riding that you might want to explore. One network of trails lies just behind the airfield to the east. This is a tight singletrack maze in a heavily wooded area. There are no mountain views here, but the terrain is varied and the elevation change is minimal. If you prefer a more spacious ride, the Mount Snow ski area has developed a series of trails and a designated riding area. The fee for trail use is $6 per day, and a helmet is required. The mountain trails are well marked, and there is even a slalom course for competition. You can take your bike up on the chairlift for a $15 fee, sparing yourself the grueling climb to the summit. At the bottom, you will find that mountain biking is also a spectator sport, as the group of regulars congregate and share stories of battles won and wipeouts endured! The subculture of off-road riders is an interesting one to join, especially for an afternoon. Refreshments, rentals, and bicycle gear are available near the base lodge.

A variety of hotels and motels can be found throughout the Mount Snow area. West Dover has one inn that is set far apart from all the others, however, as far as accommodations and dining (and unfortunately price range) are concerned. The Inn at Sawmill Farm, approximately 3 miles from the airport, is the very height of New England weekending elegance. The inn is set on beautiful grounds and its restaurant is rated one of the top ten of its type in the country. The chef is world renowned, and the experience is undeniably gourmet. Reservations well in advance are required, and the busiest season is during the fall, or peak foliage season.

If You Go:
Plan a special weekend to Mount Snow in the fall. Ask about the package deals for The Inn at Sawmill Farm, and if you can swing it financially, take someone very special there. Enjoy an afternoon walk along the nature trails behind the airport or play golf at the club. Spend some time relaxing around the inn and ask about local activities that fit to your interests.

Alternatively, plan a ski trip to Mount Snow with some of your friends. Fly in early on a spring morning and arrange in advance to use a courtesy car. Enjoy the day and stay at one of the smaller motels surrounding the base lodge. Fly home early the next morning, when you are rested and rejuvenated.

Contacts:

The Inn at Sawmill Farm
  (802) 464-8131 or (800) 493-1133
  P.O. Box 367
  West Dover, 05356

Mount Snow Airport FBO
  (802) 464-2196 or (802) 464-8481
  West Dover, 05356

Mount Snow General Information
  (802) 464-8501 or (800) 451-4211
  (lodging, mountain biking, skiing)
  89 Mountain Road
  Mount Snow, 05356

Burlington (BTV)

Location: Northwestern Vermont by Lake Champlain

Airfield: Burlington International Airport has more runway length and facilities than you will need. Despite its proximity to major mountain ranges, the ILS here is fun to fly and the approach is without significant difficulties. There is a splendid view as you fly in over the lake, so be sure to plan your visual approach accordingly. The field is shared by military as well as civilian traffic, and often I have seen F-16s departing here with their afterburners aglow. This is quite a sight.

Transportation is available from the airport, both taxis and rental cars, and the city is only a few miles away. You may want to use Burlington as your airport of entry for clearing customs from Canada. Just be sure you are familiar with the procedures and documentation necessary to do this. I had a very unpleasant experience with customs officials one evening here when I made a departure from the formal procedural protocol on my way back from Montreal. It cost me a fine, a lot of aggravation, and generated an abundance of paperwork.

Activities:
1. Cycling
2. Lakefront activities (sailing, swimming, boating)
3. Antique's shopping

Rollerblades and bicycles are two modes of useful transportation.

4. In-line skating
5. Skiing

Background: Burlington is a wonderful destination for the aviation adventurer and has much to offer during all seasons. It has many elements of a Vermont country town, but it's also the largest city in the state. As a college town, it is home base for both undergraduate and graduate programs of the University of Vermont. You do not have to travel far from the city to experience rural Vermont, either.

Perhaps the most important natural resource here is Lake Champlain, which has undergone significant successful cleanup over the past several years. There are a number of beautiful lakefront accommodations that are perfect for a weekend escape. (See If You Go.) Just at the edge of town, by the lake, is a 7 mile paved path. This is shared by cyclists, joggers, and in-line skaters, protected from traffic, and a nice place to spend a couple of hours. There is a beach, park, and several picnic areas along the way.

If you are equipped and eager to handle winter conditions, Burlington is your gateway to perhaps the most challenging mountains in the Northeast for Alpine skiing. Mount Mansfield gives rise to Smugglers' Notch and Stowe, two areas worth pursuing when

Burlington (BTV)

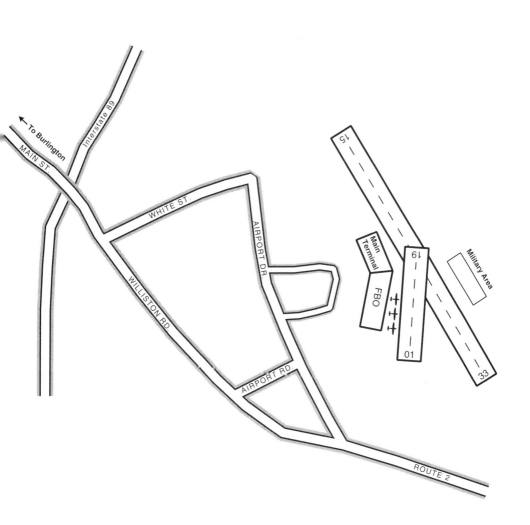

conditions are good. The terrain is steep, and the runs are lengthy for eastern skiing.

The town of Burlington has more than 100 bars and cozy restaurants. Church Street is a hot spot for shopping, strolling, and pubbing, and this region is the home of Ben & Jerry's ice cream as well! The collegiate atmosphere is pleasant and noticeable.

If You Go:
My favorite place to stay outside of Burlington is Shelburne Farms. During the summer, this is a working farm-purely Vermont. The main building looks very much like a château, and there is a small summer camp here. Periodically, in the summer, there are outside concerts and performances. The grounds are lovely, right on Lake Champlain, and the area is perfect for walking and casual exercise. The accommodations are a bit pricey in the summer months, but everything is at your fingertips here, and it really is a special place.

One of the more popular day hikes in this region is the Camel's Hump. You will see this peak as you approach by aircraft from the east, part of a range approximately 30 miles from Burlington.

If boating-in particular, sailing-is your passion, you will not be disappointed with Lake Champlain. The lake is vast and the surrounding mountains provide a beautiful backdrop. The shoreline is interesting, and there are many places to stop, lounge, and enjoy a snack or a full meal. Explore Lake Champlain by boat from one of the rental agencies, or you can take a ferry ride across the lake to Plattsburgh, New York. This is a favorite activity of mine during the fall foliage season.

Contacts:
FBO at BTV (valet air service)
    (802) 863-3626

Lake Champlain Regional Chamber of Commerce
    (802) 863-3489
    (for complete accommodation listings)
    60 Main Street
    Burlington, 05401

The Inn at Shelburne Farms
    (802) 985-8498 summer (802) 985-8686 winter

Taxi from BTV Airport
    (802) 863-1889

Ski Rack (bike rental in town near bike path)
(802) 658-3313
85 Main Street
Burlington, 05401

Earle's Bike Shop (3/4 mile from airport)
(802) 864-9197
2500 Williston Road
South Burlington, 05403

Winds of Ireland (boat rides and rental)
(802) 863-5090
at the Community Boathouse
Burlington, 05401

Basin Harbor/Vergennes (Private)

Location: The east shore of Lake Champlain, south of Burlington and north of Rutland

Airfield: Basin Harbor is a 3200-foot soft field that lies just adjacent to a beautiful lakeside resort, the Basin Harbor Club. This privately owned strip is primarily for guests of the resort. There is no FBO here, and the resort management maintains the field and provides assistance to general aviation guests. The strip is unlit, there is no fuel available, and you must supply your own tie-downs for parking. The landing surface is usually in excellent condition, but on occasion it gets too wet and too soft for use. By calling ahead (see Contacts), you can verify conditions and make plans for your approach and landing. The field uses a left-hand traffic pattern and is oriented north-south (02-20). If you are staying at Basin Harbor, a bellhop will be happy to help you with your bags to the registration building.

Activities:
1. Golf
2. Tennis
3. Swimming and boating
4. Antique's shopping
5. Maritime Museum (on-site)
6. Cycling

Basin Harbor Club, Vergennes

Background: The Basin Harbor Club is a great opportunity for a family weekend getaway. It has been in existence since the late 1800s and is family owned. Located on a beautiful cove at the eastern shore of Lake Champlain, 20 miles south of Burlington, the resort is extremely well organized and a weekend here requires very little preparation or planning. The Basin Harbor Club is open from mid-May to mid-October and is much quieter during the spring and fall. From late June to early September, there is a summer camp here that caters to school-aged children. There is so much to do with your family that you will probably have trouble relaxing, especially if you want to take advantage of all the amenities.

Bicycle, boat, and canoe rentals are all possible from the beachfront of the resort. Guided lake tours aboard a resort-owned 40-foot boat and charter fishing are also popular activities. The golf course is excellent, and package deals are enticing.

The surrounding countryside is lovely, although my favorite way to explore the region is by boat. A small outboard motorboat can be hired from the resort, enabling you this freedom and adventure. The country roads are nice for cycling, and the local area is a popular spot for antiquing. Let the hotel staff guide you based on your specific interests.

Basin Harbor/Vergennes (Private)

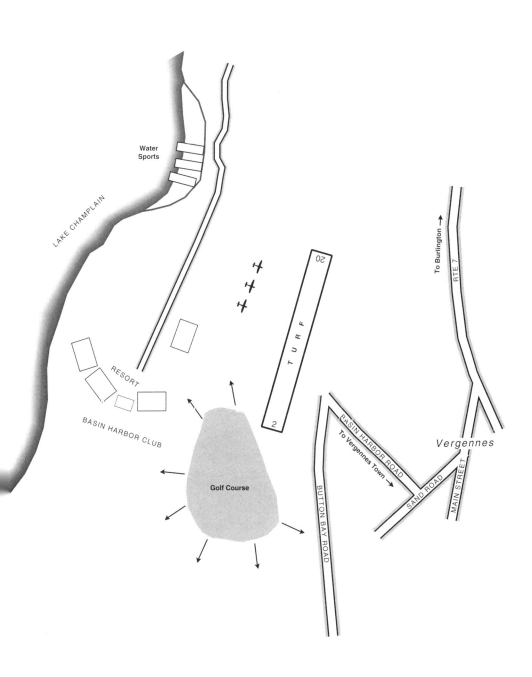

If You Go:

A trip to Basin Harbor Airfield is really a trip to the resort. If you are coming with your children, mid-summer is ideal. Although foliage season around Lake Champlain can be breathtaking in late September, early October is perhaps my favorite time. The resort will be quieter then, but you could be in for 30-degree nights. Whatever the conditions, this is a beautiful place, and you are bound to have a memorable few days.

Contacts:

Basin Harbor Club
    (802) 475-2311 or (800) 622-4000
    Box 7
    Vergennes, 05491

NEW YORK

Warren County/Glens Falls (GFL)

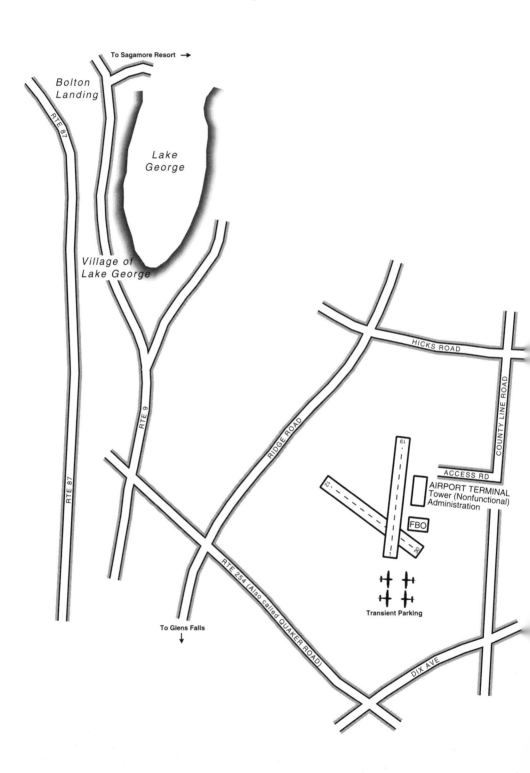

Warren County/Glens Falls (GFL)

Location: Upstate New York just south of Lake George

Airfield: Warren County is a sizable airfield with 2 intersecting runways just east of a range of the Adirondacks in upstate New York. This field was originally designed for military use and equipped with a tower, which currently is not operational. Nevertheless, it is a little airport with a big airport "feel" to it and with no congestion. Multiple precision and nonprecision approaches are available, making this place ideal for training and practice approaches. There is a Hertz Rental Car Agency based at the local FBO, but be sure to arrange for a car ahead of time. No one will be sitting at the desk unless you are expected, and the cars must be brought in from a nearby facility, several miles away. Taxi service is also available.

Activities:
1. Boating (lakefront activities)
2. Antique's shopping
3. Camping
4. Nature walks

Background: Warren County/Glens Falls Airport is your gateway to the Lake Coorge recreational area. Lake George is one of the prettiest lakes in this region. The orientation is north-south, and it connects to Lake Champlain at its northernmost point. The water is clean, the shoreline is beautiful, and the surrounding area is mountainous. There seems to be great environmental consciousness about the waters, coves, and shoreline. By taking a boat ride along the shore, you will see some lovely homes and boathouses. If you are interested in antique powerboats, you will find several prize vessels here as well. Virtually any watercraft can be rented, from jet skis to sailboats, at numerous lakefront agencies.

Camping is possible on several of the islands on Lake George. From the water, you can see picnic benches and campsites on these small, secluded islands. Several of them are big enough for multiple groups, but many are "one-family getaways."

The beauty and natural splendor of the lake are contradicted by what industry has done to the area over the past 15 years or so. Some of the small towns around the lake have been so built up that you hardly have the impression you are out of the city. In addition, there are many amusement parks and entertainment-type centers surrounding the lake. This attempt to capture and entice the week-end crowd has been effective. On a beautiful afternoon, during the season, there is traffic gridlock along the main roads. If I sound somewhat critical of this place, don't misunderstand me. The lake is beautiful and a wonderful place to spend a few days. Getting to the water may be a struggle, though.

Accommodations range from a quiet romantic bed & breakfast to a large affordable hotel. The Sagamore Resort is perhaps the most well known and exclusive major resort on Lake George. It is situated in Bolton Landing, midway up on the west shore of the lake. This spot is an opportunity to experience Lake George and relax for a couple of days. It is not inexpensive, but package deals are available, in addition to discounts in the off-season. There are three restaurants on-site. Golf and tennis are popular activities, while walking the grounds and looking out at the lake from the private peninsula/dock is perhaps the greatest asset of the resort. The Sagamore has its own rental marina for powerboats and a private beach for swimming. Three-speed bicycles are free of charge and readily available. There is a health club and a spa here, so you can pamper yourself appropriately.

Venturing away from the resort, the town of Bolton Landing is perhaps the most tasteful in this lake region. In town, there are a few stores worth browsing, but antiques can be found all along the shore drive.

If You Go:

Call the Sagamore and make reservations for a quiet weekend in mid- to late fall. You can either rent a car from the airport or the Sagamore will transport you, but they charge a fair amount for this service. Stay at the resort and rent a boat to view some of the lakefront properties. If you prefer to have some exercise, canoes and kayaks are also available for hire. Enjoy the buffet at the Sagamore's main dining room. This is featured on most weekend nights and is really spectacular. Plan a morning of golf or tennis or simply sit by the shoreline on a lounge chair with your favorite book or companion. Watch the boats go by slowly and day dream. Take a swim in this clear and clean water, but stay out of the motorboat area.

Alternatively, rent a canoe from one of the agencies in Bolton Landing, the Water's Edge. Take some camping gear and head across the lake to a group of islands northwest of Bolton Landing. This area, known as the Narrows, has several small islands that you can camp on or just walk around. Staying overnight requires a permit. (See below for details.)

Contacts:

Warren County/Glens Falls FBO
    (518) 792-5995

Hertz Rent-A-Car
    (518) 792-8525

The Sagamore Resort
    (800) 358-3585
    110 Sagamore Road
    Bolton Landing, 12814

Ranger Station (for camping on the islands)
    (518) 499-1288

Glenn Island (camping Information)
    (518) 644-3304

Water's Edge (boat rental agency)
    (518) 644-2511
    Sagamore Road
    Bolton Landing, 12814

About the Author

Dr. James Kohn is a native of Brookline, Massachusetts. He attended high school and medical school in the Boston metropolitan area and his college and surgical training have been New England based in Brunswick and Portland, Maine, and Burlington, Massachusetts. His pilot training began as a simple flight along the Maine coast and left him with the inspiration to compose this guide.